Frank Trollope

**A Woman's Error**

Vol. II

Frank Trollope

**A Woman's Error**
*Vol. II*

ISBN/EAN: 9783337071745

Printed in Europe, USA, Canada, Australia, Japan

Cover: Foto ©ninafisch / pixelio.de

More available books at **www.hansebooks.com**

# A WOMAN'S ERROR.

A NOVEL.

IN TWO VOLUMES.

BY

F. TROLLOPE,

Author of "Broken Fetters," "An Old Man's Secret," "A Right-Minded Woman," &c.

VOL. II.

London:
T. CAUTLEY NEWBY, PUBLISHER,
30, WELBECK STREET, CAVENDISH SQUARE.
1869.
[ALL RIGHTS RESERVED BY THE AUTHOR.]

# A WOMAN'S ERROR.

## CHAPTER I.

More than a month has passed since the events recorded in our last chapter, and the cold winds and rain of April had given way to the genial and bright sunshine of May.

Maud had heard nothing from home for a long time. She had finished another novel, which had realised a considerable sum. She had been associated with the most gifted men and women of the day, and they one and all admitted her great talent, and sought her society; no one more so than her respected friend Mr. Fitzgerald, who had been a frequent visitor at the Boothby's.

Augustus Boothby spent almost the whole of his time in Maud's company. Hourly he watched her, and a strange feeling filled his soul as he did so, a mighty and uncontrollable passion was stealing into his heart. He had learnt to love her with a love such as he had never felt in his early youth—a love such as can only be understood to a truly sympathising mind.

It was, as we have said, the month of May, and although there was bright sunshine and a cloudless sky the spirits of Maud were greatly depressed. She was alone in the drawing-room, trying in vain to dispel the gloom which filled her heart with grief, for in spite of all her efforts her one great sorrow weighed her down. She thought of the happy week she had spent at Pentlow Hall, in Cecil Woodhouse's company, the love she bore him and her happiness, when she fancied that love was reciprocated. She tried to cast from her these reminiscences, but she could not. She attempted to write, but could not, so she rose and paced up and down the room. At length she became calmer, seated herself at a table, and tears flowed plentifully from her eyes, for the spirit of desolation seemed to have taken possession of her soul.

The door was suddenly opened and Augustus Boothby stood before her.

"Good morning, dear Maud," he said, taking her hand and pressing it warmly; but on looking at her face he started, and said hurriedly:

"I fear I have intruded, Miss Courtenay. Have you had bad news from Bridgnorth?"

A bitter smile writhed poor Maud's lips, as she replied:

"No, I have had no news, bad or good from home. The fact is, Mr. Boothby, the 'dark mood' as the Irish say, is upon me to-day, from which I have vainly endeavoured to rouse myself. You are no doubt aware, that there are periods when a depression of spirit takes possession of us, and we cannot for a time shake it off. I am so glad you have come. I assure you, you have not intruded."

"I wish I could banish for ever from your heart that feeling of desolation which I have long known oppresses you. It is terrible to see one so young so sorrowful."

"You, I am sure, do not for a moment think the youthful heart cannot know or feel sorrow; but there are weak-minded people who maintain the young cannot feel and ought not to know sorrow."

"It must be a weak-minded person indeed, who can entertain such an absurd notion," returned Augustus, " there are thousands of commonplace people who talk of the never ending joys of youth, and whose idea of the spring time of life, as they call it, is to seek mirth and gaiety whereever it is to be found. Such unthinking people deem it unnecessary to reflect on the past, the present, or the future, they only understand happiness to consist in loving and being loved as they call it," and a sarcastic sneer curled the proud lip of Mr. Boothby.

For a minute there was a pause, when Maud, anxious to change the subject, broke the silence by asking :

"Can you tell me where to find a teacher of languages?"

"The modern or dead languages?" asked Augustus.

"The dead, Latin and Greek. I have an ardent desire to be thoroughly acquainted with both, but more especially the latter."

"You are I am sure acquainted with both languages," said her companion.

"Very slightly."

"I know an excellent tutor, to whom I will introduce you. He will bring you on rapidly. He was at college with me, but reverse of fortune has compelled him to turn his talents to account. I am truly glad to hear that you intend mastering Greek and Latin, you will make a first rate classic."

"I intend to study very hard," said Maud, "I have a particular leaning to Greek and Latin, and fancy I have capabilities that way—"

"And another way," said Augustus, smiling, and holding up one of her works.

" Oh, yes ; of course I knew years before I commenced writing that sooner or later I must do so. But, Mr. Boothby, do not all feel this— did not you ?"

" Yes, and as you say, all do, or nearly all ; but they do not all shine forth."

" To what do you attribute the failure ?" asked Maud.

" The want of education—at least sufficient education. Still in spite of this the possessor of intellect and talent feels them burning within him, causing him great bitterness and sorrow— a sorrow different to all others, one which rather embitters than chastens the spirit ; there is no humbling influence, for he feels that he is unappreciated, and that the talent God has implanted in him is lost. His must be a bitter lot."

After a short pause, Maud said :

" When I have thoroughly mastered Latin and Greek, I shall travel. I have a longing desire to visit Greece and Egypt."

"To hear you talk," said Augustus. "I fancy I am living my life over again. Every feeling that you speak of I have known. But you have this advantage over me, no one ever sympathised with me, no one understood me, whilst you have one who understands and sympathises with your every word and feeling; aye, and I may say every thought."

Again a bright ray of sunshine illumined the young girl's heart, but she spoke not. After a minute or two, Augustus, who had been gazing intently at his companion, said:

"I have more than once thought your last work was an outline of your own life. I am not of that opinion now."

Maud looked up suddenly, and said:

"No. I assure you it was not. It has been a rule of mine, and was so from the first, never to be egotistical in my writings. There is, however, no doubt that all a writer's sentiments and ideas will be to some extent promulgated, although unconsciously at the time. I will not deny that in all my works, most of the characters are taken from life and from my own observation, but in no instance have I ever alluded to myself. If a writer cannot find, either from his own study and observations on life, or in the well of his imagination, sufficient material for the incident of a more than ordinarily good novel, he had better at once give up what he considers his vocation."

"I quite agree with you, and I assure you it was only when I first had the happiness of making your acquaintance, that I thought you had sketched your own life, but such a surmise was quickly dispelled, as I became to know you more intimately. By the bye, when is your new book to be published?"

"Very shortly, I believe."

"I am glad to hear it," said Augustus. "I anticipate pleasure in its perusal."

After a moment's pause, he continued—

"Are you going to Almack's with my sister, to-night?"

"Yes," replied Maud, faintly smiling. "Julia says I must consider it a necessary duty; but, in truth, I care very little about it. I should be much happier in spending the evening at home to enjoy a little music and reading."

" Or writing," said Augustus, smiling.

" Or writing," repeated Maud.

" I can quite enter into your feelings, for they are precisely my own. I care nothing for balls, I never did, except for the study of character they afforded. I have often wondered why, even as a young man, I could take no pleasure in dancing; the opera is to me the most enjoyable of all public amusements."

"Why not?" asked Maud, as she looked into her companion's almost perfect countenance.

" Because I was never cared for, or really loved by any one with the exception of my brother and Julia, and their love was not the affection I have thirsted for. Amongst literary women I have never found one who could comprehend my peculiar nature, until I was introduced to you, Maud. *You* do I feel certain."

" I feel certain, I do," replied Maud, in a low

earnest voice, which went to the very soul of her companion.

For some time neither spoke, till Mr. Boothby began:

"I have lived many more years in the world than you have, Miss Courtenay; but there has been a strange similarity in our lives. There has been the same want of sympathy from others, the same feeling of desolation in our hearts, how severe none but ourselves can know. May God grant you may escape the *one* great sorrow I have experienced."

Maud replied not; she was thinking over the truthfulness of the first part of his speech, and pondering deeply on his last words; she knew not to what they referred. Finding his companion did not reply he continued—

"You do not care for the kind of amusement that Almack's offers. Were you always as little inclined for balls, which to the great bulk of women appear to afford such pleasure, and obtain no slight admiration from men?"

Maud looked up at her companion's face as she said:

"Admiration! what a bauble! I neither value nor expect it. I was ever too careless of my personal appearance. My time and my thoughts are always too much occupied to bestow either the one or the other, on what the world calls pleasure. If I desire approbation, it is for my writings, which I sincerely believe deserve admiration. If any one took the liberty of paying me a personal compliment, I should consider it a mere idle one, and value it as such. When I was young, my companions set me down as stupid, for I could not take delight in any of the amusements they seemed to enjoy so much; nor could I share in, or care to listen to the common-place conversations that were going on around me by the young men and young ladies, and was consequently pitied by them for my stupidity. These butterflies little knew how ardently I was seeking a congenial soul."

"You have found that soul?" asked Augustus, in a whisper and a trembling voice.

"Thank God I have!" said Maud, solemnly. "My manner was usually unconsciously to myself, cold and proud, a manner anything but pleasant to strangers, so that few liked me, and as to love, my dearest mother's is the only love I ever did or do possess."

A slight shudder passed over Maud's frame, and her lips trembled.

Mr. Boothby was on the point of pouring forth ardent vows of the passionate attachment that burned within his heart, but checked himself as he thought "my time is not yet come," so he turned the conversation and asked for some music. Maud instantly took her seat at the piano and played and sung to him, and under the soothing influence of her exquisite voice and the charming melodies she warbled, the bitterness of their spirits was soothed, and once more sunshine peeped forth in their hearts.

## CHAPTER II.

IMMEDIATELY after dinner, Lady Boothby and her young friend, Maud Courtenay, retired to their respective rooms to dress for a ball at Almack's that evening.

Maud, instead of commencing her toilette, seated herself in an easy chair before the fire, and with her feet on the fender thought over the events of the morning. In this meditative mood she continued until she was aroused by the entrance of Lady Boothby's abigail, who had come to assist in the arrangement of her toilette.

" Good gracious, Miss Courtenay, not began to dress yet?"

"No," said Maud smiling, "there is plenty of time."

"Indeed, Miss, you are mistaken, there is scarcely an hour, Lady Boothby's toilette is very nearly completed. Shall I begin your hair?"

"Yes," said Maud, as she arose and seated herself before the toilette glass.

"What dress will you put on?" asked the maid.

"The white silk."

"Where are the ornaments and flowers for your hair?" was asked.

"I wear neither."

The abigail shrugged her shoulders, and when the dress was on, she said:

"Where are mademoiselle's jewels?"

"The only one I ever wear is, suspended round my neck."

This was a small star set in diamonds.

Again the abigail shrugged her shoulders, but when Maud rose, she could not help admiring the exquisite simplicity of the whole attire.

Maud descended to the drawing-room, and in a

minute after Sir Harry and Lady Boothby joined her. The carriage was announced and they were all speedily seated therein.

" Maud ; do you dance ?" enquired Sir Harry, with a quiet smile.

" Occasionally, not very often."

" You are not fond of dancing ?" enquired Lady Boothby.

" Not very. My dislike, however, to going to balls is not so much the dancing, as having to walk about the rooms, or sit down with some empty-headed person I have danced with, who can talk of nothing beyond the charming ball he had been at the night before at the Duchess of ——, or, how he had been bored at the opera, to which he had been a hundred times ; or some crack friend who had lost a large sum on the Derby ; or his enjoyment of society in Vienna and Paris, neither of which cities he had probably ever visited."

" My dear Maud," said Julia laughing, " how dreadfully severe you are."

" No, dear Julia, only just."

"But, my love, when people meet they must talk."

"I suppose they must; but surely they need not indulge in common-place nonsense."

"Then you disapprove of dancing?" said Sir Harry.

"Not so. I dislike balls in general, but I look on with pleasure when children meet together to enjoy so healthy an amusement."

"Then it is only children of a larger growth that you think ought not to dance?" asked Sir Harry, smiling.

"Just so," said Maud gaily, "these children of a larger growth as you term them, seem to me to make such a business of dancing, but I especially dislike to see grey headed old gentlemen and ladies, fathers and mothers of families, so far forget their dignity as to go off like spinning tops in the waltz or gallopade."

"Or the polka," laughed Sir Harry.

"To me the most disgusting of all dances. Still one that at the height of its popularity every foolish old man and woman thought it requisite to be taught. I never saw it danced but I asked myself where was the boasted pride of the women of England?"

"Where indeed?" said Sir Harry, laughing heartily at Maud's comical, though true picture.

"I fear Maud's picture is too true, as regards a large number of the fashionable dancers," said Lady Boothby. "It is a pity that the youth of both sexes spend so much valuable time in frivolous amusements instead of study."

"I hope you will meet some congenial spirits to-night," observed Sir Harry, "there will be a strong gathering of the *literati* and you need not be at a loss for a suitable companion."

"I have no doubt I shall enjoy myself exceedingly. Mr. Boothby will be there, will he not?"

"Oh! yes, he will meet us."

"Then I cannot fail to have a pleasant evening."

A sudden feeling of happiness passed through Sir Harry's heart as he heard Maud ask so anxiously for his brother.

The carriage stopped, and the party entered the brilliantly lighted ball-room.

Nearly an hour had elapsed ere Mr. Boothby made his appearance; as he entered, Maud was engaged in conversation with a gentleman to whom she had been introduced. Augustus immediately joined her, shook hands with the gentleman, who immediately after left them.

"Have you been dancing, Miss Courtenay?" asked Mr. Boothby.

"Oh! no, I was more pleasantly engaged in talking to your friend, who has just left us. He is a very well read man."

"There's Julia and my brother talking to the Duke of Northwich, and Mr. Trevelyan," said Augustus. "Shall we join them?"

"Yes, if you please," replied Maud.

After the usual salutations with the Duke and Mr. Trevelyan, both of whom Maud had often met, Lady Boothby repeated Mr. Boothby's question.

"Have you been dancing, Maud?"

"No, I don't care for it, you know."

"Yes, but you should have one valse. It would raise your spirits; you are looking rather *triste*."

Maud could not conceal a smile which stole over her lips, at the idea of dancing raising her spirits, and as she smiled her eyes met those of Mr. Boothby's. A glance passed between them, and then bending down, he said in a low voice,

" I will not ask you, Maud."

She looked up quickly, and Augustus was amply rewarded by the expression in her eyes.

" Had not Miss Courtenay avowed her disinclination for dancing," said the Duke courteously, " I should have asked to have been honoured with her hand in the next valse."

Maud bowed and was about to reply, and in courtesy to accept the invitation, when the Duke said gaily,

" Ah! thank you, Miss Courtenay, I meant not to induce you to say yes. I will not be so selfish, but I shall hope to be permitted having the pleasure of accompanying you round the room, after I have fulfilled my enagagement with Lady Eustace."

Maud bowed gracefully, and accepting Mr. Boothby's arm, walked to a seat at a distance.

As soon as the dance was finished, Maud and Mr. Boothby arose, and proceeded arm-in-arm through the room till they met the Duke.

"I shall leave Miss Courtenay in your Grace's charge," said Mr. Boothby, turning to his friend, "I must go and speak to a group of friends, or rather acquaintances, I see yonder."

The Duke introduced his companion to many of his friends, people distinguished for nobility of birth as well as for for genius and talent. Men and women whom England could glory in. Not only was she presented to these high-minded people, but also to a great many common-place and frivolous of both sexes, and she noted all down in the tablets of her memory, as studies for future writings. To her astonishment, as well as to the astonishment of a great many others, she met her old friend Mr. Fitzgerald, who for some unaccountable reason had taken it into his head to go to Almack's, a place which he had not visited for many a long day.

"Well, Miss Courtenay," he said, shaking her hand warmly, "how have you enjoyed your visit to Almack's, your first, I believe."

"Yes, it is my first," said Maud, "I have found the scene a useful study; but as to enjoying the ball, or rather the dancing, I care nothing about it. These balls are mere dancing parties."

"Nothing else," returned Mr. Fitzgerald. "But tell me, do you consider they are conducive to the mental improvement of the young men and women who nightly assemble at them."

Maud looked up at the old man's face and replied,

"There is much to be said against, yet there may be points in favour of these assemblies; though to me there appears, I must confess, very few. I do not think the minds of those who seek pleasure night after night in such assemblies can become elevated. Their ideas must become frivolous and their characters weak. How piteous it is to see so many fair and pure young girls, throwing away their time and talents in such trifling and I fear often sinful pursuits. It astonishes me to see mothers aiding in the work of folly, mothers who think of nothing, care for nothing beyond getting their daughters married. How some of these poor creatures would hate themselves if the truth were laid before them. But they were educated to think that as soon as their children are educated the great object in life is to get them what is called settled, or in other words to secure a husband of some sort. Am I not correct, Mr. Fitzgerald?"

"I wish for the sake of those fair young creatures I could say you were in error; but I cannot."

"Then you agree with me," said Maud, sorrowfully.

"Yes, I consider you quite a philosopher, Miss Courtenay."

"More of a misanthrope, I fear," said Maud, with a smile, "and yet that cannot be, for I love, I adore goodness and everything that is beautiful. Look, Mr. Fitzgerald, at that lovely girl, I could gaze on her till I knew every lineament of her beautiful face."

" I would to Heaven that all women thought as well and deeply as you do, Miss Courtenay."

" No, Mr. Fitzgerald, that would never do," said Maud, smiling, " then there would be no variety in our study. Besides, I do not think that deep thinkers are always the most amiable beings in the world. In truth, I am sure they are not. By sad experience I know it." A mournful expression overspread her brow. " They become disgusted with many of their fellow creatures, in consequence of having read their shallow characters, and seen their common minds, and though they love and appreciate worth and goodness when they find it, still they discover so little of the latter, that it does not compensate for the great preponderance of the former, and thus the deep thinker becomes embittered, proud, stern, and cold to their fellow creatures, with whom they can have no sympathy."

" But, my dear Miss Courtenay, do not these

deep thinkers, like poets, in some measure, live in a world of their own creating?"

"To some extent they do. There are those, Mr. Fitzgerald, who would rejoice had they never lifted the veil and gazed on the bitter hollowness that lay beneath it. Had they passed through life, studying neither the good nor the bad; for alas! if they seek the one, they must also find the other, and become well acquainted with both."

"Are you one of those who regret studying human nature, who would blind your eyes to evil and to good, for as you truly say, we cannot seek the one without finding the other. Are you one of these, Miss Courtenay?" asked Mr. Fitzgerald, in a low voice, that none could hear but his companion.

As she replied he fixed a searching gaze upon her, but Maud answered truthfully—

"No. If I had how could I have depicted scenes and pourtrayed characters that I know to be life-like. And even setting that aside, I would not have blinded my eyes, for if I had not beheld the evil I must have lost the good. They are so intermingled."

"That's true enough; but what has been your aim?"

"To study those around, and to work in the hope of good to my fellow creatures."

"Humph!" muttered the old gentleman.

"I perceive," continued Maud, "you consider it a wild dream; but I will not despair."

"Never do so, my dear," said Mr. Fitzgerald, with a gratified look. "At this very moment your holy dream may have been realised."

They were joined by Augustus, and Mr. Fitzgerald took leave of them for the night.

"What a very beautiful girl Miss Gibson is." And he directed Maud's attention to the spot where she was standing.

Maud started on hearing the familiar name, and asked hurriedly—

"Where is Dora Gibson?"

"There she is," said Augustus, "with the

dark hair and Asiatic cast of countenance. Do you know her?"

"I see now," replied Maud. "No, I don't know that lady, but possibly my friend may be a relation of hers."

"No, that lady is an orphan, and without a relation in the world. She was born in Madras. Her father held a good appointment in the India service. She is very rich."

"She is not at all like his Dora," said Maud, unconsciously.

"His Dora," remarked Augustus to himself.

The Duke of Northwich came and asked Maud to waltz with him, and not wishing to appear particular she complied.

Maud was extremely absent, for her answers to his Grace were not only not to the purpose, but very short. He saw at a glance something had occurred to cause such great depression on her spirits, but he little imagined how far away from the gay throng in which she was moving the mind of his partner was. The faces and forms of all around her, replaced by those of Dora and

Cecil Woodhouse, and deep sorrow entered her heart as she thought of their soon becoming man and wife.

The valse finished, Augustus came to conduct Maud to the carriage.

As they drove home she scarcely spoke, a chord had been touched in her heart—a name spoken which had power to call up memories she had striven to flee from, and a train of thought had been suggested which she could not break.

## CHAPTER III.

ANOTHER month had elapsed since the events recorded in our last chapter. It is June, and the height of the London season. Mr. Boothby continued constant as ever in his daily—nay, almost hourly attention to Maud. In the month that had passed since the night of the ball at Almack's, he had often thought over the words that had unconsciously fallen from her lips, and felt that she, too, had suffered from an unhappy attachment. The very idea seemed to make him love her more ardently, for this he imagined was another link to bind them more closely to each other.

Maud, however, knew not all his feelings ; she felt an indescribable pleasure in his society and his conversation, his gentleness—nay, his almost fondness towards her, soothed her troubled heart. She felt that there was one who cared for her, and it was comfort to her yearning young heart.

It was a bright sunny morning, in early June, Sir Harry, Lady Boothby, and Maud were partaking of their late breakfast when the letters were brought in. There was one for Maud from her mother, as well as one from Ellen Raymond. Maud had not heard from any one in Bridgnorth or its neighbourhood for a considerable time. She broke the seal of her mother's letter with strange and mingled feelings, fully expecting to hear the marriage of Dora and her cousin Cecil announced; but no such decided intelligence was conveyed by her mother's letter.

After giving a favourable account of her own health, Mrs. Courtenay wrote:—

" Woodhouse and Miss Gibson are now, I suspect, formally engaged. He appears to dote upon her, and there is no mistaking the depth of her affection for him. As I do not know Dora well enough to speak to her on the subject, of course I cannot say for a certainty that they are betrothed, but, in my own mind, I am almost sure of it.

"Cecil often comes from Pentlow Hall to see me, but with the exception of asking if I have heard from you, he never mentions your name, and when I speak of you and your friends, he becomes reserved and silent, and appears as if he did not care to hear of you. Oh! Maud! had you cherished the love of that good man, instead of scorning it, he would have loved you now, as I know he did once.

"I heard from Robert; he is still with his regiment, and quite well. Take care of yourself, my darling child, and do not try your strength too much. Give my kindest love to Julia, and remembrance to Sir Harry.

"Always your affectionate mother,

"MAUD COURTENAY."

Maud re-folded her mother's letter with an almost calm expression on her face, and then opened the one from Ellen Raymond, which served in some measure to corroborate Mrs. Courtenay's surmises, for she also imagined from circumstances, partly real and partly fancied, that Woodhouse and Dora were at last affianced.

"Julia," said Maud, "you remember my cousin Woodhouse, and also Dora Gibson, who was staying with us when you were at Bridgnorth?"

"Perfectly well," said Lady Boothby smiling, and fixing her eyes on Maud's countenance. "They were attached to each other, or, at least, we all thought so."

"Yes, and they are now, I believe, engaged; at least, I hope so, for they are both good, and deserve to be happy," said Maud, with not the slightest embarrassment in her countenance or manner.

"Then my suspicions were groundless," thought Lady Boothby, as she looked into the calm face of her young friend. "Maud never loved her cousin, or she could not look and speak so completely unembarrassed."

Truly, no human being would have imagined that a fierce fire was burning in that young girl's heart, consuming and drying up every fountain of joy. It was not the engagement between Woodhouse and Dora alone that caused Maud so much unhappiness. The utter coldness which he exhibited when her mother mentioned her, name to him, and his entire apathy regarding her added greatly to her grief, and this her mother said was entirely her own fault, as he had loved her once, and had now cast her from him for ever. Oh! how deeply would the mother have repented her words could she have read the daughter's heart at that moment.

Maud sat talking with Julia and Sir Harry the usual time, till they retired to their different morning engagements. The former went to the drawing-room, where she knew she would be uninterrupted. When she got there all acting was over, the storm which had been gathering burst forth, she clasped her hands in utter wretchedness, and murmured—

"Be merciful to me, oh! God! be merciful to

me, and in Thy hands let me put all my confidence and hope and trust. I conceived in my proud heart that sorrow could not touch me. I reckoned too much on my own strength. I thought that the bitterness of my grief had passed, but I have been undeceived. Oh! God! give me strength to bear this bitter trial."

Tears streamed over her cheeks in torrents, and she hid her face in her hands. She was sitting thus when the drawing-room door opened, and Augustus Boothby entered; but Maud was in a kind of stupor, and neither heard nor saw him, till he stood in front of her and asked—

" My dear Miss Courtenay, what has happened this morning to cause you such deep grief? I trust no bad news has come from Bridgnorth?"

" Nothing, thank you," she replied, with a smile, or rather the sad mockery of a smile. " Mamma is quite well, and my brother sends good news from India. They are all who care for me."

" Not all, Miss Courtenay," said Augustus,

emphatically, looking keenly into her face, for he felt assured that her words were a subterfuge.

"I was thinking," she murmured, "that we might outlive every joy, every interest in life, and have no wish left, save that we might lie down and die, and pass away to that world where all the trials and anxieties of this life will be obliterated."

"Why not subdue such sad thoughts? Your strength—"

"Strength, Mr. Boothby, where is our strength when trials come; it only serves to prove our weakness. Yes, we imagine ourselves strong till we are tried; and then—oh! bitter is the truth presented to us, and we find how lamentably we have deceived ourselves."

"True," said Augustus, "such is human nature. We arrogate to ourselves the belief that we are possessed of more strengh to bear sorrow than we really have, and perhaps for this very reason, when the trial comes it falls heavier than if we had not so proudly trusted in our own great strength, instead of looking to a higher, a mightier power."

"Far heavier," returned Maud, with bitterness, "for desolation alone takes possession of the heart. Oh! Mr. Boothby, what then is the value of fame, or any other earthly gift?"

Mr. Boothby looked fixedly at Maud's face, there was a peculiar wildness in her tone and manner that attracted his attention, at the very moment when his heart was overflowing with love towards her.

"Miss Courtenay," and he spoke in an earnest tone, "I fear, nay, I am sure, that you suffer far more than you allow your countenance to indicate."

"You are right, Mr. Boothby; God alone knows how much I suffer," Maud replied, in a voice of passion which she could not control.

"I too, once felt as you do now," said Augustus, earnestly, "though fame even then was mine. My name was coupled with the most talented men of the day, my works were appreciated by all, but—but I was never loved. I almost hated the world, where none could understand me, and I was too proud to endeavour to make them, had it been possible. My heart became stern, and my whole nature changed by the one great event of my life, the influence of which has never passed away. I hated the world, for just then my jaundiced eye could not behold the good that was mingled with the bad. Oh! Miss Courtenay, my heart was mourning as yours is now. I then thought grief would never pass away."

"You seem to forget," said Maud, somewhat soothed, "that perhaps the deepest sorrow is caused by an investigation of our own hearts, when we discover the pride and passion that has prompted us, in an evil moment, to cast from us those whose presence made the sunshine in our hearts, and whose love being withdrawn from us, causes our after life to become cold and cheerless."

Could Maud have seen the expression of agony that passed over her companion's countenance as he listened to her words she would have been alarmed, for a fear had come upon him that she whom he had learnt to love so intensely was attached to another.

"No," he said, in reply to her last words, "I had not forgotten that; in all sorrows of the heart I believe it is ourselves who not only increase, but too often create them. But, Miss Courtenay, I did not make that sorrow of my youth which caused me for a time to hate life. My mind was jaundiced, and no wonder. It was not my lot to dwell in the midst of God's nature. I mean the pure and open country, where I could worship and reverence Him in every blade of grass. No, I lived in the midst of fashion, and having had one bitter taste of the heartlessness and worthlessness that lies beneath society, I studied every mind and character that came under my notice, and oh! God forgive me! how I scorned those votaries of fashionable life by whom I was surrounded."

"Once," said Maud, "I thought that the sorrow you speak of would be the heaviest I should ever know, for bitterly have I mourned over the world's hollowness and deception, its frivolity, its neglect of high and holy things. Mr. Boothby, I would not have my fellow-creatures study life as we have done, unless, like us, they could appreciate and love all that is good, holy, and beautiful as we do. Herein at least is compensation."

A long and painful silence ensued, each being buried in his or her own thoughts, until Sir Harry entered the room. Maud was sensitive in the extreme, and almost feared that the baronet would see in her face the anguish and desolation of her heart. So with a mighty effort she roused herself to speak to him with gaiety; but Augustus was not to be deceived; he knew her manner was assumed, and he deeply commiserated her. He longed to tell her of his love. that she might be assured she stood not alone in the world— that having suffered, as she had, once, he could sympathise most truly with her, and would soothe her troubled spirit—watch over—protect and love her through life.

## CHAPTER VI.

THE month of June is drawing to a close, not so the gaieties of the London season. Belgravia continues her whirl of excitement with unabated zest. One bright morning Maud begged that her breakfast might be served in the bed-room, as she did not feel quite well. With the breakfast was also brought a letter bearing the Bridgnorth post-mark, but she merely glanced at the outside, letting it remain unopened till the servant had left the room, for her heart told her that it contained news that would pain her. She commenced her breakfast, and as soon as she had finished, rang the bell for the servant to take away the tray, at the same time requesting that she would let her know when luncheon was ready.

No sooner had the servant closed the door than she broke the seal of her mother's letter, and the first few lines were these:—

" Your cousin, Cecil Woodhouse, is at last formally engaged to Dora Gibson. He told me this himself."

Poor Maud's eyes became fixed upon the words which she read over and over, and for some considerable time she sat gazing on the letter, as if all power of speech or thought had been taken from her. At length, with a deep drawn sigh, she let the letter fall on the table, and a torrent of tears rushed down her cheeks. She cried as if her very heart would break. After a time, and when the heavy weight on her breast seemed lightened by the tears she had shed, she raised her hands and cried in a tone of terrible anguish—

" Oh! my God, I thank thee that I am permitted to know that the fond hope I have so long and secretly cherished can now never be fulfilled, and oh! God forgive me for my pride and haughty bearing towards him. I pray, fervently pray, that this union may be productive of every happiness to them both."

Again she took up her mother's letter, which was full of reproaches for her daughter's conduct to her cousin Woodhouse. There was considerable justice in her mother's remarks, she owned, as she recalled her coldness to Woodhouse, her pride, her haughtiness, her stern, unbending conduct, which she felt had not only uprooted every particle of love from his heart, but every feeling of brotherly affection; Maud felt that, and again she implored the Almighty to bless him.

Maud wrote a short letter to her mother, and a loving one to Dora Gibson, congratulating her on her engagement to Mr. Woodhouse, and wishing them both every happiness. No sooner, however, had she folded and sealed her letters, than the full force of her desolation returned with renewed force. No tear dimmed her eye, but a wild and unnatural excitement took possession of her, and she paced up and down the room, her hands pressed firmly to her aching head. Her lips were deadly pale, and in the centre of each cheek was a small red spot. Her dark hair was thrown back from her face, and a strange expression rested on her whole countenance.

A gentle tap on the door arrested the thoughts that crowded on Maud's brain, she smoothed her ruffled hair and seated herself before the dressing table, as she said—

"Come in."

The abigail stared in amazement as she saw Maud still in *déshabille*, saying—

"Luncheon is on the table, miss."

"Indeed! I had no idea it was so late."

"It is nearly three o'clock."

"I will be ready in a few minutes."

The girl's eyes caught sight of the letters Maud had been writing, and she asked if she should have them posted, which Maud begged she would.

In a few minutes Maud had arranged her hair and made her toilette, and having bathed her eyes and her temples, with a calm countenance entered the dining room, and greeted both Sir Harry and Lady Boothby with unusual gaiety.

Conversation was carried on during luncheon with great animation, neither Sir Harry nor his wife having the slightest idea how that gaiety was forced.

As soon as luncheon was over the ladies went for a drive, and it was the general remark of those they met, how unusually animated Miss Courtenay appeared. They little thought that in every lively sally and gay laugh there was a dash of bitterness that sprung from her very heart's core.

"I am glad to see you so gay, Maud," Lady Boothby said, as they returned home from the drive. "I hope you will be quite well and equally in spirits in the evening, for my party will be one of the most brilliant of the season."

As Lady Boothby had said, her assembly, a few hours later in the day, was one of the most gorgeous of the season, not only was it graced by a prince of the royal blood, but the highest nobility of England, and commoners the most wealthy— in fact, wealth, rank, intellect, youth and beauty were all congregated in that brilliant throng.

Amongst the aristocracy of talent, however, Augustus Boothby and Maud Courtenay were most prominent.

In the course of the evening, as Augustus and Maud were standing talking, the former said, as he bowed to a fair girl who passed—

" There is one of the very few here present in whom I take an interest. Do you like her appearance ?"

" If I may judge from her countenance," returned Maud, " she is no ordinary being. Who is she ?"

" Her name is Lockhart. She is an orphan, and her only relation is a widow, very rich, and, as you see, moving in the first circles, but a woman of very common mind, and one on whom her niece cannot bear to be dependent. That girl, Maud, possesses only thirty pounds a year. She is well educated, and is desirous of obtaining a situation as governess; to this her aunt strongly objects, as being derogatory to her position in society, and she is quoted as a good and affectionate aunt. considering that she has several daughters of her own. In public she is everything that is kind; but in private she leads her niece a terrible life. Her great objection, however, is that she considers it a degradation for one so nearly related to her to be in a subordinate position, and, consequently, throws every impediment in the girl's way of obtaining a suitable situation. Miss Lockhart is not to be daunted in her determination. Her greatest trial is to be dragged to these places, these scenes of gaiety, in which she takes no interest."

"Oh! there are those," said Maud, "who delight in crushing the sanguine hopes of the young; who love to awaken them from their daydreams, and cause them to despair."

At this moment Maud perceived a lady approaching, of the most splendid beauty. She appeared about eight-and-twenty years of age. She was leaning upon the arm of a gentleman some three or four years younger than herself. "Who is she?" was the general question, denoting that she was a stranger.

"That is the Countess of Cavendish; the young

man with her is the Honourable Mr. Tennant. That middle-aged man, just behind her, is her husband. They have been married six years, and have ever since resided abroad. They arrived from Florence about a week ago. Is she not gloriously handsome? That young fellow on whose arm she is leaning, and who has been with them a good deal in Italy, evidently thinks so."

This was said by a gentleman close to Maud, who was just going to ask Mr. Boothby who the beauty was, and if he were acquainted with her, when her eye rested on his countenance, and she was astonished at the strange expression thereon. He was ashy pale, his short lip curled with pride and scorn, and his eyes shone with an unnatural light, as he looked upon the approaching beauty, on whose face, as she bowed to Mr. Boothby, was a proud, defiant look of mocking scorn. The salutation he acknowledged haughtily, and also returned the look of withering scorn.

As Mr. Boothby turned away from the sight of the Countess, his eyes met Maud's, and a total change came over his countenance—in the place of scorn, love, reverence, and devotion shone forth. He saw that she read him aright from the look of indignation she cast on the beautiful countess, and he said, in a voice of sadness—

"Maud, dear," it was the first time he had called her so, "pity her, while your high soul scorns her; for truly she, like too large a portion of the world, is an object that you, in your philanthropy, must mourn for. Yes, pity, while you scorn and loathe her, for glorious as is her outward beauty, there is black and fearful deformity beneath."

As Augustus ceased speaking, he stood erect, a stern, proud expression upon his face.

"Yes," said Maud, looking kindly at him, and speaking in a gentle voice, "yes, we must mourn for and pity her. This is all we can do. We must leave the rest in the hands of a higher power."

"True, Maud, true."

When Maud retired to rest that night, or rather morning, for it was long after midnight, she thought of Augustus and the suffering he had endured through the hypocrisy and deceitfulness of the scornful beauty she had seen that night. All her musings tended to draw her heart nearer to the man who, she felt convinced, was the only one who had ever understood her.

## CHAPTER V.

THE following morning when Augustus came to Portman Square, instead of going to the drawing-room, as he was accustomed, he went to his sister's morning-room, where he found her engaged in reading some abstruse German works, for Lady Boothby was not a mere frivolous woman of fashion, but one who read much and thought more.

"My dear Julia, I know you will pardon my breaking in upon your studies," said Augustus, shaking her hand warmly.

"Why make any apology. You know how glad I am to see you at all times."

"I am going to make an audacious request."

"What is it?"

"That you will put aside your books and give me your attention for half-an-hour."

"Willingly, *mon cher*," said her ladyship. "Judging from your countenance, you must have something important to communicate."

"It is of the greatest importance to me."

"Indeed! What is it?"

"I am betrothed."

"To whom?"

"To Maud Courtenay."

"To Maud Courtenay!" repeated Lady Boothby, as a curious expression passed over her countenance. "Engaged to Maud Courtenay did you say? Did I hear you aright, Augustus?"

"Most assuredly you did. That is a subject on which I could not jest. Why question the truth of what I stated?"

"My dear Augustus," said Lady Boothby, gravely, "is it possible you can have forgotten Edith Ryan?"

"Edith Ryan!"

"Yes, it is scarcely a year since she was here, and surely then you sought to win her love."

"Never," said Augustus, looking up proudly, "nor did I ever love her."

" Not love her! "

" No. I was pleased with her society for a season. Her great beauty charmed me, and her gentleness and truthful character attracted me to her side. There were times, perhaps, when I fancied my respect for her might have ripened into a deeper feeling. But, Julia, charming as was her society, and beautiful as was her face, there was wanting—"

"The great intellect you have discovered in Maud," said Lady Boothby. "Was not that the case, Augustus?"

"Yes," returned her companion. "But, Julia, do not for a moment imagine that I cannot admire and respect Miss Ryan's character still. In truth, she appeared like an angel of truth and purity to me, compared to the frivolous women by whom we were surrounded. At length, however, I have found the one my soul has long thirsted for, one who can sympathise with me in my most ardent aspirations. Maud Courtenay is a kindred soul, a woman of intellect, and possessing not only the rare attributes that few women attain, but she has a delicate mind and a pure, noble nature. But, Julia, I do not class Miss Ryan with the frivolous, laughing nonentities; far from it. But she is not a deep thinker. She reflects only upon things that may happen to herself or her friends; of those of the world — the mystery of life — she knows nothing."

"But she is not devoid of cleverness," put in Lady Boothby.

"Certainly not; but she cares not for studies of a profound nature; she would not be capable of them. I doubt if she ever leaves this visible world—I speak allegorically. Her imagination is not expansive or high, though her character is beautiful. There are few men who would not have loved her intensely. Mine is a strange, proud nature. Perhaps she was too gentle, too good for me."

As he said this, an almost imperceptible smile, approaching the expression of a sneer, curled his handsome lip; but a sterner, prouder look came over his face when Lady Boothly said, in a peculiar tone—

"Edith is a lovely creature, and her character is as beautiful as her face."

"Her character, I have already said, is truly beautiful, and her mind is refined and delicate; but there is nothing approaching greatness or sublimity in it; and lovely as she is in some respects, she is of a widely different class to my Maud. You perceive at once the measure of Miss Ryan's mind, and the things it contains, while Maud's runs still and deep, and few, very few there are in the world capable of knowing and appreciating her. I must leave you now, Julia. I was anxious to apprise you of my engagement, that you might look upon Maud in the light of a sister. Will you do this?" and he rose to take leave.

"Why ask such a question," said Lady Boothly, rising from her seat.

"Because I feared, from the early part of our conversation—"

"I was mistaken as to your intentions and your heart; now you misunderstand me; but you ought not. I thought you knew me better. You know how I respect and love Maud, and will love her as a sister. When I was speaking of Edith, and my admiration of her, I was not alluding to her understanding. Neither did I, for a moment, think of comparing her to Maud. Indeed, I should deem it an act of injustice to class her with any of the women I have ever met; for with genius and talent, she has a rare and delicate mind. I consider a great intellect and high genius the most beautiful of God's gifts, far above mere amiability of character. This latter loveliness, Augustus, you appear apt to forget."

The poet smiled, as he said, rather bitterly:

"None can admire and love beauty of character more sincerely than I do, and have done from my very childhood. But, my dear Julia, the woman I would select for my wife must possess more than character; she must have mind and genius far above mediocrity. Even she who enthralled me in early youth, she possessed splendid talents, but her mind was of a common order; that I knew not when I offered to marry her, for she had descended to the most trifling stratagems to hide her real character and sentiments from me. I was a foolish boy then, and was won by a beautiful face. I must go now. Thank you for your kind promise of loving my Maud as a sister."

Mr. Boothby went direct to the drawing-room, where he found Maud reclining upon a couch. Her eyes were closed as if in sleep, and her mouth, usually so scornful in its expression, wore a sweet and placid smile, while the long dark lashes, resting on the pallid cheek, gave a look of almost meekness to the countenance: a study for a sculptor would that young girl have formed. He would have loved to gaze upon the broad brow which proclaimed itself as the pure high temple, within which the light of splendid genius shone. There was a look of great languor upon her countenance, and her skin was dry and burning. She heard not Augustus' approach, and her thoughts were far away. At length a weary sigh escaped her lips, her eyes slowly and heavily unclosed, and she saw Augustus standing beside the couch, earnestly regarding her.

"How are you, my Maud?" said Mr. Boothby, as he respectfully raised her hand to his lips.

"Quite well, Augustus, thank you. I felt inclined for a morning's idleness, so I closed my eyes to shut out external objects."

"Do you think you have been idle? Your eyes have been closed, but your brain, I know, has been active."

"How long have you been here?"

"Nearly an hour."

"What, standing by this couch?"

"No; I have been only a few minutes in the drawing-room. I went direct to my sister's morning room, as I was most anxious she should know of our engagement. I need not tell you, Maud, that she has promised to love you as a sister—but here she comes."

The next minute Maud was embraced by her

friend Julia, who welcomed her as a sister. She did not remain long, as she was called out of the room by her own maid. As Lady Boothby left the room, Sir Harry entered.

"Harry," said Augustus, leading Maud towards his brother, "I think I need scarcely ask you if you will receive Maud as your sister. She has promised to be my wife."

A flush of pleasure passed over Sir Harry's face as he said, affectionately:

"Yes, my dear Augustus, gladly will I receive her as my sister, and I pray God that you may both be happy."

As he spoke he raised Maud's hand to his lips, and then replaced it in that of his brother; as he did so, an earnest expression settled on his countenance, and for a minute he appeared to be offering up a prayer to God that His blessing might rest upon them. It had been the earnest wish of Sir Harry for months past that Maud might become his brother's wife.

## CHAPTER VI.

The evening was most lovely, and the assemblage of rank and fashion in Hyde Park was unusually large. Augustus rode by Maud on one side, and Sir Harry on the other. Lady Boothby was a little in advance, with Mr. Briggs, an intimate acquaintance of the Boothby's. Maud had been conversing with her companions in a lively strain, when suddenly she said in a somewhat peculiar tone:

" How remarkably happy and contented, or rather I should say, amused, all these people look. What an animated yet stereotyped smile there appears on every face! It seems to me that this necessary duty, this daily canter on the same spot, must in time grow exceedingly irksome. Yet one and all seem as amused and interested as though they were only this day initiated into the gay scene."

"Poor things! it is their training," replied Augustus, whose lip was slightly curled. "You surely have discovered, my dear Maud, that in civilised society it is considered a breach of good breeding to be, or rather to appear, otherwise than intensely happy; and such is the high value they set upon the world's opinion, that those who are wretched strive and struggle painfully to attain a gay and happy expression of countenance; there are several apparently the gayest here whose histories I well know. But in justice to a few, I must say that there are those who cultivate the appearance of gaiety from other and purer motives than the value of the world's opinion; there are those who dare not let a shadow rest upon their features."

"That seems strange," said Maud.

"Yes; but it is so."

"I understood the art of masking before

coming here," said Maud, "and I know it is not in human nature that out of so vast an assembly none should be sad. But is it not lamentable that 'society,' as it is termed, should demand smiling faces, even though the heart be bursting with anguish."

"It is, indeed, most painful," said Augustus; "but are we not all generally acting a part? There are some natures always must be to a certain extent, Maud."

"I know it," she replied.

"Augustus," said Sir Harry, "here is Maxwell coming, and, I suppose, his wife."

A lady and gentleman, both well mounted, were approaching. A bow only was exchanged between the gentlemen, for they had not been on intimate terms.

"Who are they?" asked Maud. "The lady is strikingly handsome."

"A Mr. Maxwell and his wife; they are just married, and are going on the continent to live, where the lady's beauty will ensure them a footing in society they cannot obtain here. The young man has nearly broken his father's heart by this marriage. His family came over with the Conqueror, and the girl is the daughter of a tradesman in the city; she will be very rich, and has had a tolerably good education, but—but Maxwell should not have done it. He had not the right feeling—I will not call it pride—that his father had."

" Then he cared not for intellect in a wife so long as she had money?" observed Maud.

" Yes ; he is one of those men who had rather that his wife did not possess intellect," answered Sir Harry.

" But did not his father make objections to the match?"

" He had not the opportunity. They were married before he knew of the acquaintance. The marriage was a secret one, and Maxwell calls it ' a clever stroke of diplomacy.' "

" Good heavens! what a mind—what tastes the man must have!" cried Maud.

" The coarsest of the coarse," observed Augustus. " He has been one of my studies. Many would have passed him by as worthless; but I have turned him to some account, by studying him, for to understand human nature thoroughly, both the good and the evil must be studied. We must be acquainted with every class and order. I have not exaggerated the man's character."

"I am persuaded you have not," replied Maud, "I have studied character, and seen evil as well as good, but have never found them wholly separate. There is no heart so black that a white spot does not dwell in it;—there is no person on earth so utterly worthless and abandoned that a spark of truth is not in him."

"True, very true, Maud," said Sir Harry, earnestly.

"Sir Harry," Maud asked, "is it right or is it wrong, or is it a matter of no importance, that a man or a woman of good blood, as it is called, should marry with a person in a lower grade of life?"

"Opinions differ on this subject," replied Sir Harry; "perhaps I am too much on the side of keeping the pure blood untainted. But there is a large amount of hypocrisy on this subject. It is not the pride of birth that the generality of people care for; it is a far lower thing—gold! Wealth is their ambition, and in ninety-nine cases out of a hundred that is the highest they have ever known. Now, had I a daughter I would sooner see her married to the true-born gentleman (provided, my dear Maud, he was a gentleman in mind as well as birth), though he had to work for his daily bread, than the low-born man, though he possessed riches and lands unbounded. I say lands, for these grovellers always purchase land on retiring from business. I pretend not to judge for others, or to say whether such marriage be right or wrong; but my spirit, or pride if you like, would not permit me to form an alliance with a plebeian. I can admire and reverence beauty of character and nobility of mind, regardless of the possessor's origin—I speak of either sex—but if it were a woman, I could not marry her. I should look up at the faces of my ancestors in the picture gallery with a feeling something akin to conscious wrong to their time-honoured race and name."

Maud looked in Sir Harry's face and saw the short lip curled with pride, and at that moment his whole expression of countenance was like his brother's.

" I quite coincide with your ideas," said Maud. " Where was there ever a *mésalliance* in a noble family that it did not prove the first step to its downfall ? When did a man of good blood ever wed a woman of low origin, that in after years his children did not almost curse him. Many would condemn me for these sentiments, but for this condemnation I care not. Let them probe their own hearts and see if wealth is not their idol. Which is the lowest aim for parents to seek in marriage—gold, or equality of birth ?"

" The answer is obvious," said Sir Harry. "I do not consider it wrong to preserve an ancient name from sinking. I would not, Maud, have you misunderstand me. You must not think I entertain the vulgar notion that equality of birth is the only requisite in marriage; far from that—love, respect, a reverence for nobility of mind, wherever we find it."

"Augustus," asked Maud, changing the subject, "do any of these fashionable people ever dare to take a canter in other directions from this? I should soon get tired to death of such an absurdity. If I lived in London I should always be longing for the moors and the sea shore. How can you always live here?"

"I am here only during the season, and am always glad when that comes to an end. Did not business compel me to visit London I should go abroad again. Maud, I should like to take you to the Holy Land, and other notable places that I have visited—to Switzerland, to Italy, where we could commune more closely with the great Creator."

"That was once my dream of purest happiness —to wander over the world with a companion who could enjoy it with me. How my soul has thirsted to visit the Holy Land, and gaze upon the ruins of bygone splendour. Augustus, that was a dream too bright and beauteous ever to be realised."

" Why so, my love ?" said her companion, with animation. " Why should we not go there together."

" Yes, Augustus; for you to guide me over that hallowed land will indeed be to fulfil my most ardent wishes."

At this moment Lord William Freeman, a handsome, but brainless young man of fashion, and immensely conceited, joined them. He was so affected and opinionated, and gave himself so many airs that to a stranger he would have been mistaken for the son of a wealthy city merchant who had lately retired from business with an income of thirty thousand a year and his " place" in the country. Lord William, we have proved, was the exception to his class.

" Where are you going to-night, Miss Courtenay ?" asked the young lord, in an affected tone.

" To Lady Fortescue's," replied Maud.

" Oh ! a literary *soirée*. Bah ! I never patronise such sort of places."

"Indeed! I am astonished," said Maud, with a slight sneer. "Perhaps you prefer studying at home."

"Home! Oh! dear no. It's very rarely that I allow the light of my countenance to shine at home. I carry my wit in other directions than home."

"Where?" asked Mr. Boothby.

"Oh! to various places, my dear Boothby. To-night to the opera."

"We go there before attending Lady Fortescue's *soirée*. I fear the music will so rivet our attention that your wit will fail to divert us, should you visit Lady Boothby's box."

"Very likely," replied the young man, languidly. "You are very new."

"Dreadfully so," Maud replied.

"Why, Miss Courtenay, you are quite a philosopher. I should have thought you had studied Epictetus."

"So I have," said Maud with a smile.

"Why you are—"

"What?" asked Maud.

"As great a—a—well as great a blue as Lady Mary Wortley Montague."

"Do you not study the best classic authors?"

"Not I; my chief study is dancing and ethics," replied his Lordship.

"Good morning, Freeman. We must join Lady Boothby and my brother."

Lord William and Maud bowed, and they separated.

"I pity that young man," said Maud.

"Poor shallow-pated coxcomb," returned Augustus.

Vast numbers of the gay throng were leaving the park, but the Boothbys continued their ride, as the cool of evening was making it very pleasant.

"I quite enjoy the breeze," said Maud, "from some cause or other I feel excited."

"Yes, to my mind the park is more enjoyable than when it is so thronged."

"I suppose the passing and repassing such multitudes of people has made me dizzy."

"We will return to Portman Square," said

Lady Boothby, seeing Maud's face flushed, and a strange brilliancy in her eyes.

* * * * *

"Who is that beautiful girl in the opposite box," asked a fashionable-looking young man of a companion.

"Don't you know?"

"How should I, seeing that I have not been in England for the past two years."

"Ah! I forgot. That is the celebrated novelist, Miss Courtenay."

"Is that Miss Courtenay?" said the first speaker. "By Jupiter! she's very handsome. What a splendid complexion, and how strangely bright and expressive her eyes."

"Have you read her works?"

"Yes, and think them immensely clever."

"Yes, for one so young. She is scarcely more than one or two and twenty."

"She is very *distingué* looking. What do you think of her, Fitzgerald?" he asked, turning round to an old gentleman at his back.

"Miss Courtenay," replied the old gentleman,

"as far as regularity of features are concerned, is decidedly not handsome, but her whole bearing is striking and expressive. Her eyes are beautiful, and her mouth singularly expressive. There are many who differ with me. They see so much pride in that curved upper lip; but if ever genius shone forth upon a face it is there. I have no doubt you, as well as many others, think her looking very handsome to-night, for her eyes have not their usual mournful expression, and her complexion, which is usually pale, is now very brilliant—I was going to say unnaturally brilliant. There is a very strange look about her."

"That is Boothby, whose poems took the world by storm, is it not, in the box with Miss Courtenay?"

"Yes, I must join them very soon, as I go in their carriage to Lady Fortescue's."

"I have read Miss Courtenay's works," said the young man, "and I think them brilliant sketches of life. In her last novel I could not help thinking the heroine was, to a great extent, her own life."

"Such, however, is not the case. One evening, in joke, I asked her if it was not so, and she assured me it was not, said that she disliked egotism in an author; and from my knowledge of her, I have not the slightest doubt that her answer was the truth."

Mr. Fitzgerald accompanied Maud to Lady Fortescue's, and had a good deal of talk with her during the evening. He remarked that there was a wild brilliancy in her eyes, and an unusual degree of animation in her manner, and when he took her hand in his to bid her good-night, it was parched and burning. He little imagined that the delirium of fever was even then upon her, lending such a strange fire to her eyes, and so bright a flush to her cheek.

Immediately on her return to Portman Square she retired to her room, telling her friends that she intended writing to her mother. It seemed almost like instinct that she should do this, as if she felt the delay of an hour would take from her the power of discharging this duty. So, after taking off her ball dress and putting on her dressing gown, she wrote to Mrs. Courtenay as follows :—

"MY DEAREST MAMMA,

"I am about to communicate to you something that I trust will not only be pleasing to you to hear, but which will meet with your hearty approval. In my letters I have often mentioned Mr. Augustus Boothby with the highest respect, both for his talent and honourable character. He has for some time paid me marked attention, and has at length offered me his hand in marriage, which I, on my part, have accepted. At length I have found the treasure my heart has thirsted for—one who can understand and enter into all my feelings and sympathise heartily with me. Augustus loves me truly, deeply; and I am affianced to him in the sight of Heaven. All I now require to complete my happiness is your blessing, my dear mother."

Having sealed her letter and placed it on the table, she commenced undressing. She felt a strange, reckless gaiety in her heart, and on looking at herself in the glass she almost laughed aloud as she saw her flushed, heated face and wild eyes. She retired to bed, and sank into a restless sort of forgetfulness, for it could not be called sleep, and as the night wore on the fever increased, and she awoke, but not to consciousness. Delirium came on, she laughed and talked incoherently, the intense pain in her head caused her face to become suffused with a deep crimson, whilst her hands and lips were parched and dry.

As Maud did not make her appearance at the breakfast hour, Lady Boothby ordered her abigail to go to her room and enquire if she were unwell. In a minute or two after the young woman had left the room a fearful shriek was heard, penetrating even to the breakfast-room. Lady Boothby rushed upstairs, followed by her husband. At a glance her ladyship saw that her friend was raving in the fierce delirium of fever.

In the course of ten minutes the most eminent physician in London stood by Maud's bed. He looked gravely and anxiously on the poor girl, for his experience taught him that if she escaped from the jaws of death it would be almost a miracle.

Lady Boothby, after the physician had given his instructions as to the treatment of his patient, was on the point of leaving the room, when she perceived Maud's letter directed to her mother. She took it with her, and sent it at once to the post-office. She deemed it better not to apprise Mrs. Courtenay of her child's sudden indisposition till some more definite opinion had been expressed by the physician.

## CHAPTER VII.

We must now take a retrospective glance over the months of Maud's absence from Bridgnorth, and disclose the sayings and doings of some of the other personages of our story. As Mrs. Courtenay informed her daughter, Cecil Woodhouse is engaged to Dora Gibson, an event which caused some little talk in the immediate neighbourhood, and to none more surprise than to Woodhouse himself, who had loved Maud so devotedly.

He had, since Maud left Bridgnorth, spent a good deal of his time with his friends, the Raymonds, and when he visited them he always called at the Gibsons, who generally spent the day at the vicarage. Then Dora was constantly thrown into Woodhouse's society, who, as our readers will have seen, entertained a warm and tender regard for her, as a friend, nothing more. Her gentle manner, her intellectual conversation, her extreme youth, and her beautiful face, drew the young man towards her at the time bitter grief was in his heart, and the kind and gentle manners of the sweet girl soothed his troubled spirit.

But in his wretchedness, which he was for ever struggling to bury in his own breast, he never for a moment thought he was endangering the happiness of another. Sorrow—alas! too often makes us selfish for a season, and Dora little thought that Woodhouse loved her not. Time went on, and he continued his attentions to her, but never told her that he loved her, causing every now and then a sudden pang and fear to enter her heart, which was soon speedily dissipated by the affectionate earnestness of his manner.

Weeks passed, still no protestation of love

was uttered, and, in spite of all her efforts, Dora's countenance wore a thoughtful and troubled look, which was not unnoticed by her friends, the vicar and his wife, as well as by her mother.

One evening, soon after Dora had left them, Mrs. Raymond said to her husband—

" Don't you think, my dear, that Dora looked very sad to-night?"

" Yes, Ellen; lately I have frequently observed the anxious expression on her young face."

" She loves Woodhouse, I am convinced, and certainly he has done his best to win her affection. Even before Maud left home, months ago, his manner was marked towards her. I wonder what reason he has for not—" and she paused.

" For not coming to the point at once, and ask Dora to be his wife," said her husband, smiling.

" That he loves her I think there can be no doubt," said Ellen.

" If he does not he has trifled with her, and that I never could believe of such a noble minded fellow as Woodhouse."

" Nor do I believe he could act so vile a part,"

said Ellen. " His proud spirit would revolt from anything so unworthy."

" A thought has struck me, Ellen; do you think his circumstances are as good as they appear? May he not have some temporary pecuniary embarrassment. We must not judge by appearances, and it is possible that he may not feel himself in a position to marry."

The colour rose to Ellen's cheeks, and she replied somewhat indignantly—

" I do not think that can be possible; besides, my dear, even supposing that to be the case, why did he not think of that before. Why did he endeavour to win Dora's love, if he were in such circumstances that prevented his marrying. Is this your opinion of Woodhouse. Do you think him one of those selfish beings who first do all in their power to win a woman's love, and then, and not till they have succeeded in doing so, discover they are too poor to marry. Cecil Woodhouse, I feel certain, is not one of these commonplace, selfish beings. He is—he must be too noble for that."

"I believe he is, my dear," said the vicar, "if I may judge of him from other matters—nay, I am sure he is, and I make no doubt he will soon propose for Dora."

The morning after this conversation between Ellen and her husband, Woodhouse came over for the day, and Dora and her mother dined at the Vicarage. In the evening they all went for a walk. Mrs. Gibson and Ellen and her husband walked on, while Dora and Cecil Woodhouse lagged far behind, engaged in earnest conversation, but no word of love passed Cecil's lips, and Dora's young heart felt as if it would burst when he talked of going abroad a month or two hence for a few years.

The expression of poor Dora's countenance was so strangely sad, that Mrs. Gibson noticed it with alarm when they joined the rest of the party, nor did it escape the observation of the vicar and his wife.

After their return from their walk, Dora sang and played, and Woodhouse sat as one entranced, for it soothed his sad heart; and long and earnestly he talked with the young girl, but still no word of love was spoken by him.

The next morning Woodhouse left soon after breakfast. Mr. Raymond had been attending a sick man living at some distance, and did not return home till late. On his way back he called at the Gibson's; Dora was sitting by the window, her face wearing an expression of intense sadness, such as he had never seen there before. In truth, a terrible fear had taken possession of her — a fear that Woodhouse did not love her—that all these months she had been deceiving herself. Her beautiful eyes were filled with tears, which flowed over her cheeks.

Thus did Mr. Raymond find her. She dashed away the tears at his entrance, and forced a sickly smile to play around her lips, which did not, however, hide the sorrow so marked in her countenance. The vicar, at the moment as he looked in the face of the sorrowful girl, felt great indignation against Woodhouse, for being the cause of such unhappiness to a young, guileless being. Poor good-hearted man! He thought not how unconsciously it had been brought about. He formed a resolution at the moment, for though Dora strived hard to conceal her grief, she could not succeed in hiding the intense anxiety or pain that lay deep in her heart.

"Poor dear child," thought Mr. Raymond, as he rode homewards; "she is sad, because she thinks Woodhouse does not care for her now that he has won her pure young heart. Poor child! how ill and careworn she looks. She has no father, no brother; but I will take the place of a brother. It is requisite Woodhouse should know the mischief he has done. It's a delicate matter, but I will do it. Dora must no longer be trifled with; she shall not, if I can prevent it."

So soliloquised this kind-hearted young clergyman. But he forgot in his zeal for his young friend, how overwhelmed with shame she would have been could she have guessed what he was about to do. In his hot haste to carry out his intentions, he thought not of consulting his wife, if he had she would have urged him not to take the step he meditated, but at once went to his library and wrote the following letter to Mr. Woodhouse:—

"My Dear Woodhouse,—

"You will, I trust, forgive the almost unwarrantable liberty I am taking in writing to you on a subject of a delicate and private nature, and I shoud have deemed such an interference unwarrantable if my interest in Dora Gibson was not that of a brother, and had I not felt sure you love our amiable and beautiful young friend. I have seen for a long time your affection, and the preference you have shown by seeking her society, and, I believe, winning her whole heart's devotion. She has never breathed a syllable of her love for you either to Ellen or her mother, but both have noticed your unvarying attention to her whenever you met, and the affection she evidently feels towards you. We have all witnessed with pain, for the last two or three weeks, the feeling of sorrow that has overshadowed her brow, and weighed heavily upon her heart. This, I feel sure, arises from a fear that your feelings towards her are changed, or that she has miserably deceived herself. If I thought this, I should never have written this letter, but I hope I know you too well to believe that you could trifle with a woman's heart. You may have some reasons for not declaring your love for Dora; if so, pray frankly tell her the feelings you entertain towards her, for her health is evidently failing from some secret sorrow, the nature of which sorrow is patent to us all, although, poor girl, she strives hard to conceal it.

"If you love her, Woodhouse, let her hear it from your own lips. Believe me, that in taking this step, I believe it to be to your own as well as Dora's interest. I feel it to be a matter of great delicacy, and consequently, none but myself, not even my wife, have been consulted, or have the faintest idea of my intentions.

"Believe me,
"My dear Woodhouse,
"Yours faithfully,
"J. RAYMOND."

It was late when the letter was finished, but the vicar, late as it was, went out and posted it, as he wished it to go by the morning mail. It reached Pentlow Hall about mid-day. Woodhouse was in his morning room when the letter bag was brought to him. He commenced reading another letter which came by the same post, and when he had perused its contents he broke the seal of Mr. Raymond's letter, and as he read the whole truth burst upon him. Unknowingly and unintentionally he had won and had seemed to seek to win a girl's love, whom he cared not for, except as a good and gentle being, whose tender kindness of manner soothed his troubled spirit.

"Good heavens! what have I done?" exclaimed the sorrow stricken man. "How utterly selfish I have been in thus destroying the happiness of this sweet child, to whom I fled to soothe my heart which was wrung by Maud's icy coldness. What Raymond says I now for the first time feel to be true. I sought Dora constantly, and have unintentionally won her affection. This is terrible, for my love has been given to another."

For a considerable time Woodhouse sat with his face buried in his hands, and he moaned audibly, evidently in much sorrow. At length rousing himself from his torpor, he rose and gave utterance to his thoughts.

"No, she shall not think her love uncared for, mine must be the sacrifice, my utter selfishness deserves it. This very day I will endeavour to repair the wrong I have unintentionally done. This very day I will ask her to become my wife, and it shall be my task through life to guard and cherish her. Poor Dora! I wish I could love her, but that I fear can never be, save as a dear kind sister, but that she shall never know. I will, by God's help, do my best to make her life a happy one, for, undeserving as I am of her, I know and feel she will soothe and cheer my sad and weary heart."

Woodhouse raised his eyes to Heaven, and offered up a silent prayer for strength to perform what he deemed his duty. He rang the bell, and when the servant entered, he ordered his horse to be saddled and brought round as quickly as possible. He felt that delay might be dangerous, and that selfishness might again cause him to do further wrong to the suffering Dora. His horse was soon ready, and with a heart ill at ease, Woodhouse rode off at a brisk pace. Instead of going to the vicarage, as was his wont, he put up his horse at an hotel, and at once proceeded to the Gibsons.

It was evening, and a lovely one it was, to which a fresh breeze gave a more than ordinary charm.

As Woodhouse opened the garden gate, and proceeded up the gravel path, he saw Dora sitting by the window, with an open book upon her lap, but she was evidently not reading. Her pale cheek rested on her little hand, and her thoughts were of him, who was now approaching her. He walked rapidly up to the door, and enquired if he could see Miss Gibson. The servant informed him what he already knew, that she was in the drawing-room alone, Mrs. Gibson having gone to the vicarage. He walked firmly upstairs, with his lips compressed from the mighty resolution he had formed, and approached Dora, and now that his attention had been roused to the fact, he saw with feelings of intense sorrow the fading cheek and mournful expression of her eyes.

"What a blind and selfish idiot I have been," he thought. "But I will repair the wrong, and do my utmost to remove the weight from her young heart."

"Dora," he said, as he took her little hand in his. "I am glad I have found you alone, for I want to talk seriously to you. I shall not be deemed presumptuous when I say that I feel certain of having gained your confidence, and I have learned to regard you as a dear and precious friend. Dear Dora, may I be permitted to call you by the tender name of wife? Will you give me the right of protecting you through life, and guarding you from all evil. Dora dearest, will you be my wife? Tell me, will you—do you love me?" He spoke rapidly as he drew her towards him. "Speak, Dora!"

"Yes, Cecil; I love you very, very dearly," was the frank but lowly spoken reply. It was all she said, but her look of intense love, as she raised her eyes to his, answered him more eloquently than words, however impassioned, could have done.

In about half an hour Mrs. Gibson returned, and Woodhouse asked her consent to the engagement, which she joyfully gave. Woodhouse urged Dora to fix an early day for the wedding, but Mrs. Gibson objected to this, declaring that her child was too young to marry for a year at least, little dreaming what were the feelings that prompted Woodhouse to ask for a speedy union.

It was with a sinking heart that he heard Mrs. Gibson's determination, but his resolution had been thus far carried out, the sacrifice had been partly made, and with a noble firmness he determined it should be fully accomplished. He spent the rest of the evening with the Gibsons, and left just before ten o'clock for the vicarage, where he knew he should be welcomed, and have a bed provided for him. As he approached the house, he saw his friend standing at the front door, smoking his cigar.

"How are you, Raymond?" Woodhouse said, with a forced cheerfulness in his manner. "I am come to beg a night's lodging."

"And heartily glad I am to see you, my dear fellow," said his friend, shaking Cecil's hand warmly, "for it assures me that you did not think I took an unwarrantable liberty in writing as I did to you."

"Not at all," said Woodhouse. "You were quite right. I had delayed too long in asking Dora to be my wife."

"And you intend—"

"Not intend doing so, I have not only gained her consent but Mrs. Gibson's sanction also."

"I am delighted to hear this, my dear Woodhouse, and congratulate you on the beautiful and amiable wife you will possess. You will of course not mention my letter to any one?"

"Most assuredly not," replied Woodhouse. "It is I alone that can have ever the pleasure of thanking you for it—and its happy consequences."

"Come in, my dear fellow. I am anxious Ellen should be told of your engagement."

They proceeded to the drawing-room, and Mrs. Raymond welcomed Cecil gladly, and when her husband told her of the engagement she congratulated him heartily.

About a week after Dora's engagement, Woodhouse was sitting by her side, for he had been an almost daily visitor, when she said:

"I have had such a kind letter from Maud. How highly she speaks of you—of your goodness. She seems to know you so well."

"She has known me from her childhood," replied Woodhouse, whilst his heart felt well nigh bursting, as his affianced bride read several passages from Maud's letter.

With a violent effort he mastered his feelings and spoke kindly of his cousin.

That evening Dora felt inexpressibly happy, for Maud's letter had filled her heart with joy, and wretched as Cecil felt, he concealed it so well that none guessed he was not happy too.

## CHAPTER VIII.

Mrs. Courtenay was sitting at her breakfast table, reading a newspaper and enjoying her coffee and toast. The servant brought in two letters which the postman had just delivered. They were from Maud and Lady Boothby. She opened her daughter's first, and her astonishment was very great when she read the contents announcing Maud's engagement to Mr. Boothby. At first Mrs. Courtenay felt annoyed that her daughter should have betrothed herself without consulting her in the matter. However, having read Maud's letter, she proceeded to peruse Lady Boothby's, and there she saw her future son-in-law spoken of in the highest terms as a man noble in every respect. Julia also spoke of his devoted love for Maud, and concluded by hoping Mrs. Courtenay would give her consent to the engagement, and that Mr. Boothby intended writing to her in a few days.

"Well," soliloquised Mrs. Courtenay, "it is all very well and satisfactory as far as the description of this young man goes, but I must consider it strange that Maud did not write to me before and tell me something about him, and how she liked him. As it happens, Cecil Woodhouse is engaged, so I don't see any use in objecting to this engagement. I am glad to find Maud can love, for I almost began to think there was no such thing in her nature, I will write a kind letter to the dear child, and to Julia, and give my consent."

Mrs. Courtenay's soliloquy was interrupted by the entrance of Woodhouse.

"Is that you, Cecil? I am so glad to see you," said Mrs. Courtenay.

"I trust you are well?"

"Yes, and I suppose I ought to be supremely happy."

"What has occurred?"

"Oh, something that will surprise you as much as it has done me," said Mrs. Courtenay, taking up the two letters. "Maud is engaged to—"

"Engaged!" repeated Cecil.

"Yes, engaged to Mr. Augustus Boothby! You may read both the letters if you like," and she thrust them into Cecil's hand.

He felt he was bound to read them, and having done so, he said:

"I am glad to hear that dear Maud has at last found one who can understand and love her."

There was a peculiar tone in his voice, almost amounting to bitterness, but it was unnoticed by his companion.

"Lady Boothby gives a most pleasing description of Maud's lover. In the literary world he is well known and highly appreciated. I trust your daughter has met with a man capable of appreciating her genius, one who can thoroughly sympathise with her every aspiration."

"I don't exactly know what she means by

sympathy, as she speaks of it," said Mrs. Courtenay.

"She means one who can understand her peculiar nature, one to whom she can unreservedly pour forth all her thoughts, and know and feel they are comprehended."

After conversing for a quarter of an hour upon other matters, Woodhouse rose and said :

" I am going into town, so must wish you good morning. Give my kindest regards to Maud, and tell her that from my heart I wish her every happiness."

Instead however of going into Bridgnorth, he turned back and retraced his steps to Pentlow Hall, and having arrived there went direct to his library and threw himself on a couch, burying his face in his hands, feeling as if the burden of life were too heavy for him to bear.

\* \* \* \* \*

Mrs. Courtenay having written and despatched her letters to Maud and Lady Boothby, put on her bonnet and shawl, and proceeded to General

Ryans, to convey the important news of Maud's betrothal, knowing how anxious they were to hear anything that tended to the happiness of her daughter, but little dreaming what a fearful blow she was about to inflict on the sensitive heart of poor Edith. On arriving at the house, she was told by the servant that Miss Edith and the General were alone in the drawing-room. She entered and found the latter sitting in an easy chair, and his daughter on an ottoman beside him. She was reading to him. He held her disengaged hand in one of his, it was, in truth, a mighty love that bound together that father and his child.

"I am afraid I am interrupting you," said Mrs. Courtenay.

"Not at all, my dear friend," said the General, rising and shaking Mrs. Courtenay's hand warmly. "We are both glad to see you."

"Have you heard from dear Maud to-day? I think you must—you look so full of news," said Edith, with a pleasant smile.

"Yes; I am indeed 'full of news,' as you say," replied Mrs. Courtenay.

"Good news, too, I trust!" said the General, in a cheerful voice.

"Yes, good news, and news that will, I think, please and astonish you both. Maud is engaged!"

"Maud engaged!" cried both father and daughter.

"Ah! I thought I should surprise you. I was very much surprised myself. I had not the slightest idea of her being attached to anyone."

"Indeed!" said the General, smiling; "I am glad your dear child has found one whom she can love, and who who will be her protector through life. I feel sure it is no ordinary man who has won her affection!"

"You are quite right, General," replied Mrs. Courtenay; "from a description of him I have received this morning from Lady Boothby, he must be a very superior man. He is a great poet —just such a man as Maud would be likely to fall in love with. He is Sir Harry Boothby's brother!"

"I heartily congratulate you, my dear friend, and am truly rejoiced to hear the good child has made so suitable a match,"cried the General," and trust the gentleman will prove worthy of her."

Edith seemed as if she did not exactly comprehend Mrs. Courtenay, and with as steady a voice as she could command, asked :

" What is the gentleman's name?"

"Mr. Augustus Boothby," replied Mrs. Courtenay.

" Are you quite certain of the name ?"

" Of course, my dear. Sir Harry has no other brother. Here is Maud's letter, if you would like to read it."

" Then may every happiness be theirs. Maud has won the love of a good and truly great man."

That was all the stricken deer could say. She felt a deadly sickness creep over her, as if the hand of death was grasping her trembling frame.

Mrs. Courtenay rose, saying :

"I must leave you, General, for I have several things to do in the town."

The father and his child were alone.

"My dear Edith, how pale you look," said the father.

"I don't feel quite well," replied Edith.

"I am going for a short walk—will you go with me? I think it will do you good, dear child."

"No thank you, papa, not this morning. I don't feel well enough."

"Poor darling! You look as if you had a headache. Sit down, my love, till dinner-time. What a fragile plant it is," he said, patting her cheek as his eyes filled with tears.

Poor Edith! her father left her, little suspecting the true cause of her exceeding paleness. She threw herself upon a couch, where she lay to all appearance calm; her face was pallid to an unearthly degree, and her white hands were crossed upon her bosom; her eyes were closed and the long lashes rested upon her cheeks.

There she lay like a stricken deer. Hope and trust and confidence had kept her up for months, but all these had now been ruthlessly torn from her bosom, and desolation and despair had entered, excluding every ray of light—Augustus was engaged to another !

It so happened that on the very day Mrs. Courtenay received Maud's letter, announcing her engagement with Augustus Boothby, and after her visit to General Ryan, Mr. Raymond called while the General was absent. He went with the intention of asking him and Edith to go and stay with him and Ellen for a week or two, but finding poor Edith apparently so ill, he thought it would be better for her not to leave home at present, or at least for a day or two. He went to Mrs. Courtenay's, and induced her to promise to go by the evening coach to the Vicarage, and stay a week or two with him and his wife. She had been there only a few days when she was taken suddenly ill and was confined to her bed for some time. This illness unfortunately happened just at the time Maud was attacked with the fever, and the letter Lady Boothby wrote to Mrs. Courtenay, to tell her of Maud's state, did not reach her till her daughter was out of danger.

## CHAPTER IX.

We return to the mighty Babylon.

Lady Boothby had been unremitting in her attentions to her friend Maud, and had nursed her with a sister's tender care. For the first week the poor girl was delirious; now raving and throwing up her hands, as if in the fiercest agony, and anon, singing one of her songs, in a most pathetic tone, a placid smile resting on her countenance. Then for hours she would lie in a state of stupor, neither speaking nor moving. Every means were used to lessen the violence of the fever, and when, at length, it was subdued, the patient was reduced to a mere shadow of her former self. Night and day Lady Boothby watched by her bedside, till, at length, her strength failed her, and she was obliged to give up her post to an experienced nurse.

Lady Boothby was not one of those mere fashionable women, who shine only in the ball-room, the opera, or the park. During Maud's illness, she neither received company at home, nor went into it elsewhere, but devoted all her energies to her suffering friend. Mr. Boothby had scarcely left the house except at night, generally past midnight, and was there again long before breakfast time. At the crisis of the fever he had stayed all night, expecting every minute to be summoned to take a last look at the dying girl. Day after day he sat in speechless agony in Sir Harry's library, for none entered there except conducted by his brother. Now the great affection existing between these two men showed itself. With a woman's tenderness and delicacy, Sir Harry endeavoured to soothe his brother, not console him—his own heart told him that would be in vain—but he led him to look forward with hope and gladness, even should the suffering girl be taken from him in this world. Pale and cold as the marble busts around him sat Augustus, his damp hands pressed to his aching head, and with closed eyes, shutting out the light of day.

At length one night, when silence reigned throughout the house, when all but himself and the watchers had retired to rest, he heard a quick step approaching the library. His mind worked up to a state of almost frenzy by suspense, fear, and want of rest, Augustus started from his chair with a suppressed but agonized cry. He saw his brother enter the door at the further end of the large room, and walk quickly towards him. Augustus moved not; intense fear seemed to paralyse his limbs, for he imagined that his brother was the harbinger of death. Swiftly Sir Harry approached, and, taking his brother's cold hand, cried—

"Augustus, my dear fellow, the crisis is past, and the doctor says, with great care she may not only live, but in a short time be out of danger."

"God be praised!" was all that Augustus could utter, for so great was his emotion, that had not Sir Harry held him, he must have fallen to the ground. Sir Harry led him to an easy chair, and seeing how fearfully exhausted his brother was, procured some brandy, which he made him swallow. After a few minutes Augustus was persuaded to take some rest.

\* \* \* \* \*

Let us look once more upon Maud's countenance, and see the change that three weeks' illness has created there. She has only left her bed-room for the first time, and been carried to Lady Boothby's boudoir. The day is lovely, warm, and balmy, and a refreshing west wind wafted the delicious odour from the beautiful plants, placed in the windows. Sir Harry and his wife were doing everything in their power to make the invalid comfortable, by propping her with soft pillows. After a time they retired from the room, and Sir Harry went direct to the library to summon his brother to an interview that he knew he was so ardently and so anxiously wishing for. In a couple of minutes he was at the *boudoir* door, which he softly and carefully opened, and went swiftly towards the couch on which Maud was reclining.

"My beloved Maud, my treasure! Thank God, for His great goodness and mercy in again restoring you to me," and he clasped her to his heart.

Maud's bosom was filled with joy, her eyes expressed all that she wished to say, but she was too weak to speak, and Augustus had been forewarned not to allow her to talk.

"My Maud!" he said passionately, yet softly, "I know all you would say, but you must remain silent until you gain more strength. To-morrow, I hope, I may be permitted to remain longer with you, but now I am forbidden to stay more than a few minutes," and with a fond kiss he left her side just as Lady Boothby re-entered the room.

Day after day Augustus was by Maud's couch, reading to and talking with her, and in the evenings Sir Harry and Lady Boothby joined them, the latter singing and playing, thus soothing the invalid and charming her senses.

Maud had received kind and affectionate letters from her mother, expressing how much happiness it afforded her, to hear she was progressing so favourably towards restoration to health, her greatest regret was not being able to see her, for although much better, she was not sufficiently strong to be able to leave Easton.

Lady Boothby, also, had received a letter from Mrs. Courtenay, full of grateful expressions to Sir Harry and herself for their unbounded kindness to her child, and Augustus was gratified by a very kind and affectionate reply to one which he had written to her. Thus far all went on well and happily.

August had arrived, and Maud had been out for a drive in the park, but she found the exertion too much for her.

Change of air, the physician told Sir Harry, was of much more importance than physic, and that quiet was also essential to his patient's recovery.

"Do you think she could travel by easy stages to Bridgnorth?" asked Lady Boothby.

"Certainly not," replied the physician, "for the next month or six weeks she must not attempt such a long journey. She may go with you to your country seat in Berkshire."

"Then that can be speedily arranged," said her ladyship, joyfully, "the change will do us all good."

It was resolved that the following week the whole party should start for the charming county in which Sir Harry Boothby's family seat was situated.

## CHAPTER X.

It was one of those charming evenings for which the month of August is celebrated in England, when the Boothbys approached the end of their journey. They had come in their own travelling carriage, deeming it more easy for the invalid than the noisy railway, and certainly much pleasanter. Maud completely enjoyed the drive, for each object of interest was pointed out to her by Lady Boothby, who was thoroughly acquainted with every hill and dale they passed.

"Now, dear Maud," said Sir Harry, "you will soon be at the end of, I fear, this fatiguing journey, you can see the park gates."

In a couple of minutes the gates were thrown open by a grey-headed old man, who had lived in the family many years, and who stood, dressed in his best clothes, ready to welcome his master. The lodge was most picturesquely situated, on the edge of a dense wood, its front covered with creeping plants, and the garden surrounding it filled with roses, fuschias, geraniums, and almost every other flowering plant. This charming spot caught the eye of Maud, who expressed her pleasure, but when the carriage emerged from the splendid avenue of forest trees into the broad drive, with the park stretching as far as the eye could see; on one side hill and valley met her eye, and a complete sea of waving woods on the other. This sight appeared perfect bliss to her imaginative mind, her eyes sparkled, and a bright colour suffused her wasted cheek.

"Oh! Augustus!" she exclaimed to Mr. Boothby, who was sitting beside her. "Surely I have dreamt of this beautiful place. It seems so familiar to me. Those waving woods, the vast park stretching as far as the eye can reach in lovely glades and hillocks, a perfect Paradise for the mind to dwell in. Every tree, every spot seems like the face of an old familiar friend!"

"No doubt they do, dear Maud," replied Augustus, "your fertile imagination has pictured just such a spot. We don't always require to see a place with our external eyes, and when we look upon it in reality it seems scarcely more real than when we imagined it in dreamland."

"What you say is perfectly correct."

The carriage approached the fine old baronial mansion, with its castellated turrets and towers, its deep oriel windows, in all of which there was much to arouse the sensitive mind of Maud, and to fill it with exquisite imagery. At the back of the house, at a short distance, dense woods were seen, adding to the solemnity, if we may use the expression, such as to create in a refined mind an intense appreciation of its quiet poetical solitude.

Maud, occupied in looking around her, could not speak, but she was reflecting deeply, and her heart throbbed in thankfulness to the Maker of the loveliness around her.

The carriage stopped in front of the mansion; the door was already open, and the old and valued housekeeper, with the upper servants, were all assembled to greet their much loved master and mistress, and " Mr. Augustus," as they always called him.

Maud was assisted to alight by Sir Harry and Augustus, and heartily welcomed by her friend Julia to their country retreat. As it was getting late, and Maud was greatly fatigued, Lady Boothby ordered refreshments to be brought to the bed-room which her friend was to occupy, and she bade Sir Harry and Augustus goodnight. With a happy heart she sunk to sleep.

Maud had spent a happy week at ———, and not only had her spirits revived, but her health was considerably improved; she had not gained sufficient strength of body to be enabled to walk far without a supporting arm, but that of her affianced husband was always ready.

It was a lovely evening, about ten days after their arrival in the country, that Maud and Augustus went out, and strolled farther than usual. Every step they took was replete with beauty, and it was with intense appreciation that those two beings, so imaginative, gazed upon it.

"Augustus!" cried Maud, enthusiastically; "no wonder your poetry is filled with exquisite imagery—no wonder that the spirit of God's grand creations is visible in all your works."

"Yes, dear Maud, to the lovely scenes around us, to these wonderful works of the Creator, do I owe in a great measure, if not entirely, the success I have achieved."

"How you must yearn for such scenes as these when in the heated saloons of fashion. I can now fully comprehend how your genius expanded into such perfection, taught as it has been in the true school of nature. It is here and in such scenes as this you have been inspired to describe in such exquisite language the glorious sublimity of God's magnificent works."

For a short space Augustus made no reply to Maud's gratifying appreciation of his talent, which he knew was heartfelt. He was perfectly convinced she would have scorned to have uttered the words of praise had she thought otherwise.

Those few but sincere expressions of his beloved Maud, had called forth feelings that all the homage of the world and the laudations of the critics had failed to create, and his eyes glistened with a holy and sanctified joy as he looked upon his companion, and with a warm pressure of her hand replied—

"A thousand thanks, dearest girl, for your more than kind words—words far more precious to me than the praise of the whole world. They will give me new energy, new strength to work, and I trust, for your sake, I shall yet produce more noble themes. I never cared to be applauded, not even in my boyhood, but your praise is precious to me—yes, dearest, precious as the bright sun of day, as the sweet, invigorating aspect of nature. From your lips alone do I care for approval."

"Augustus," said Maud, "henceforward we shall pursue the noble path of literature together."

And a holy joy seemed to pervade her mind as she spoke.

"Yes, dearest," replied our hero, "not only in our native, but also in classic lands, in the realms of the *ideal* as well as the *actual*. Yes, in each and every path we will journey together."

"Ah! Augustus," said Maud, "how different is the influence of nature over you to what it is over some. Indeed, there are many it never seems to influence at all. Many who see no beauty beyond the actual, and very little in that. They look on splendid trees, the growth of ages, as pretty things enough, but whose only value in their estimation is the money they would fetch if felled to the earth. They cannot behold beauty in every leaf and blade of grass. The splendid old trees do not speak to them of former ages. How different it is with you who have been taught by their influence on your imagination to commune with the great Creator."

"But, dear Maud," said Augustus, smiling, "do you think that nature, mighty as is her power, can endow us with genius, or bestow upon us talent and understanding?"

"No, most assuredly not," replied Maud.

"God alone can do that. But what I mean to say is, that to the man or woman to whom God has given genius the solitude of nature is sure to call it forth."

" Do you think it necessary to resort to these places to draw out the genius of man?"

" No; but I think what I term the solitude of nature weans the mind from earthly things. Do you not agree with me?"

" Yes, entirely. No doubt the author whose mind has been tutored in the school of nature is by far the most heart-stirring writer."

" To prove the truth of that, I need only mention Milton, Thomson, Goldsmith, Spenser, and others of the highest order of genius."

" And Byron?"

" Yes: he spent his childhood amid wild and beautiful scenery, which, I feel certain, had an influence over him through his whole life."

" It was well for the world that his childhood was spent in your 'solitude of nature,'" said Augustus with a smile, quoting Maud's words.

" Ah! you may smile at my words; you not

only feel they are true, but have proved them to be so."

" How so ?"

" By throwing into your poetry the very spirit of nature, and by leading your readers, or rather I should say the minds of your readers, to pure and lofty reflection, by the charm your poetry possesses. Posterity will feel its influence."

" And will not posterity feel equally the influence of your writings ?"

" No. The world calls me a novelist, and novels have not the power and influence of poetry."

" That may be true of the great bulk of novel writers, but in your case it is not. You sketch from life and from your own deep study and observation of it; and believe me, Maud, novels such as yours will have as much influence on the readers as poetry of the highest order can have."

They were silent for some time, lost in their own thoughts as they gazed around them on the sun which was just setting over the thick forest of trees that rose up like an array of dark giants against the horizon—and on the sky which was of that peculiar red that art can never imitate.

At length Maud spoke.

"Oh! how cold and hard the heart must be that would not be full of gratitude and love to the Great Creator for giving us loveliness like this to gaze upon."

"It is in truth magnificent," answered Augustus. "Look at the lovely evening star. Not a breath stirs the leaves, and all around is wrapped in an intense stillness."

"Augustus, you know not how, night after night, I have looked upon that evening star, and longed to soar up to it. Yes, above all others it seemed as a beacon to lead me on, and cheer me on my path through life."

"And God will bless you and does bless you with that guiding star."

Again they were silent and intent upon the scene around and above them.

## CHAPTER XI.

The month of August had passed since the Boothbys and Maud arrived at ———— Park, and part of September had gone by ere it was arranged that Maud should return home. Her health was greatly improved, and Mrs. Courtenay had written to request that the whole party should accompany her daughter to Bridgnorth, to remain as long as they conveniently could. Mrs. Courtenay was, of course, anxious to see her intended son-in-law, as well as to make the acquaintance of Sir Harry.

The evening preceding the day on which they were to leave for Bridgnorth was as beautiful as it was possible to conceive, and the whole party sat enjoying their tea with the windows open, for although it was the month of September the weather was extremely mild.

As the servant was removing the tea-tray Augustus said—

"This will be our last night in this lovely spot, Maud, let us take a ramble through the park. The evening will be very light."

Mr. Boothby turned to the window and pointed to the moon, which was just rising in all its subdued glory and softened splendour above the thick forest of trees. Maud had her bonnet and cloak brought to her, and in a few minutes she and Mr. Boothby went out.

They strolled leisurely through the park and the more confined parts of the grounds till they came to the park palings, and passed through the gates a short distance to behold the hills and glades of greensward stretching far away before them and bounded in the distance on either side by the grand old forest trees.

"Maud, dearest, what makes you look so much more pensive than usual?" asked Mr. Boothby as he gazed on his companion's sorrowful face, which she took no trouble to conceal, the expression was so habitual to her, although for the last two months a strange and unnatural joy had filled her young heart and given an unusual lustre to her eyes and a colour to her cheeks foreign to them.

"I am sorrowful to-night, Augustus," she replied, in a saddened tone, "and why I am I cannot tell, unless it be that I am mourning to leave this paradise—a spot such as I never before beheld, except in dreamland. The knowledge that I am looking upon this exceeding loveliness for the last time has no doubt caused a feeling of sadness, or something akin to it, to pass over my spirit."

"My dear Maud, why do you say you look upon this lovely scene for the last time," cried Augustus, with a feeling of uneasiness. "I hope we shall have very many opportunities of coming here."

"I cannot tell why I used those words."

"Yes, love, I trust we shall often spend many weeks and months here, for have we not promised my brother and Julia that we will be their guests for a long time after our return from distant lands. Why then should you speak as if you were never again to behold this dear old place?"

Augustus little thought that on the mind of his affianced bride there was a presentiment that they *both* stood on that spot for the last time.

"We may not, Augustus," she replied, gravely. "How can we dare to say we shall survive another year."

"But we may hope that we shall," said Augustus.

"True, we may hope so; but I don't know how it is," she said, " that I always involuntarily experience a feeling of something like solemnity— I cannot call it sadness—on leaving a place where I have sojourned for any length of time. How much more, a spot of such peculiar beauty and grandeur as this; and," she added, in a tone of almost her old bitterness, but which Augustus noticed not, "a place where I have spent the happiest hours of my whole existence!"

Augustus had not the slightest notion what sadness took possession of her heart as she uttered these words, which sent a thrill of joy through his heart, as he answered, fondly taking her hand and kissing it—

"Heaven grant, my dearest girl, that you may spend far happier ones after we have looked together upon the splendour of distant lands, and stored our minds with a greater knowledge. Then, Maud, we will return to this lovely spot and labour together for the benefit of our fellow-creatures."

After some further conversation regarding their projected tour, Augustus suddenly asked—

"Maud, when do you expect your brother will return from India?"

"Not till next spring," replied Maud. "Why do you ask?"

"I should so much like to have seen him," returned Mr. Boothby; and then he added in a peculiar, half playful tone, "are you very fond of him?"

"Very," Maud replied, somewhat gravely; "as fond as it is possible any one being can be of another between whom no feeling of sympathy exists. My love for my brother is something more than natural instinct, for I prize and love his good qualities; his heart is truly noble, but —but—"

"But what, dearest?"

"I had no sympathy from him."

"Dear Maud, had you no one who could understand and sympathise with you—none with whom you could claim kindred?"

"None," said Maud.

Her lip quivered at the memory of that time before she had found that congenial spirit now at her side. A sharp pang shot through her heart as she thought of one other that might have done so.

"Poor child," said Augustus, musingly, "how strangely similar has been our fate. My brother can sympathise with me in many respects, but not in all can he understand me. Maud, do you think love cannot exist if perfect sympathy is wanting between two souls?"

A flush overspread the girl's countenance as she replied—

"There is no rule, but of this, however, I feel convinced, that where there is no sympathy there cannot exist true love. Perfect sympathy is a treasure very rarely met with. Before I knew you, Augustus, I never spoke of myself, for that would have been termed by the unsympathising persons around me egotism, but to you I cannot help expressing the thoughts that have been pent up within my breast from childhood. Oh! you know not how through life I have been misunderstood."

"Did your mother misunderstand you, like the others?"

"Yes, but do not blame her. She would have been the first to reproach herself for her injustice had she comprehended my true motives, or understood the real means of giving her assistance I contemplated. But after all, perhaps I was selfish, for the labour that enabled me to render her that assistance was, with me, a labour of love; in fact, the happiness of my life. This unsympathising spirit of my mother arose not from want of affection, for I know her love for me is unbounded, and mine for her is, I think, stronger perhaps than that of most daughters. She has innumerable good qualities. But the cord that binds us is not sympathy; that, dear Augustus, I never met with till I knew you."

"Oh! Maud, I can indeed understand how bitter must have been your feelings."

"When I condemned the common-place conventionalities of society, often and often have I been upbraided for my *outrée* opinions and, as others considered them, extraordinary ideas."

"It is refreshing to meet with one being whose sentiments differ so widely, so entirely, from the frivolous, heartless women with whom one is obliged to associate in the fashionable world, where a certain set of ideas or rules regulate every action. I suppose your friends, as well as your relatives, considered your expressed opinions erroneous."

"Yes, I was often much pained by their remarks, though they did not alter my opinions or prevent my thinking. When I was appealed to I believed I was right to speak candidly, and express my real sentiments, rather than follow in the beaten track of those who mingle in society and obey its rules, and who become mere slaves to its routine. I pitied my opponents who had not studied life as I had done, nor had they penetrated beyond the surface of what they saw, and therefore I was termed bold."

"You were right, dearest, quite right in not shrinking from giving expression to your candid and real sentiments. Had you shown wavering or timidity, it would have been unworthy. I despise that system now so prevalent, nay, I may almost say, so general in society, of women concealing their true opinions for fear of what the world may think. There is too much stiffness and too many conventional rules to allow of a feeling of good fellowship, kindness, and sympathy."

"I don't recollect at the moment," said Maud, "who it is that says the great fault of society is, that every one endeavours to mould themselves, their habits, and their ideas to one model—one set of opinions. We meet with nothing fresh—nothing original. Throughout there is a sameness, a sort of great family likeness, a similarity stamped on every person forming a part of civilised society."

"True, quite true," observed Augustus. "When I have looked on, in a crowded room, and seen the bye play where the strict rules of society are observed, I have pitied the pure in heart, yet weak in mind, who could neither speak nor act, fearing the censure of that society to which they were unconsciously mere slaves, trembling, dreading to disclose their purer, nobler sentiments, because they differed from the narrow and precise rules which had been inculcated in them as part of their education. Oh! Maud, when I have observed this state of things, how I have wished that every heart could be exposed, and that all might read the truth. How much has conventionalism to answer for? What selfishness and wickedness, what sin, what hypocrisy it disguises."

"Yes," said Maud, "there is unhappily too much truth in what you say. Still certain rules are requisite, which rules should be respected."

"No doubt; but the unnecessary and prudish codes of propriety, especially as regards the conduct of ladies; those it is that to me are so disgusting."

"And not less so to me," said Maud; "were they not so absurdly exaggerated, there would be more real friendship in society, less falsehood and hypocrisy. I have seen women who scorn the world's hollow praise or blame—act as their noble hearts prompt them, depending on their purity and loftiness of motive."

"What a sad thing it is," said Mr. Boothby, "that the sophistry of society drive its votaries to have recourse to those unnecessary and exaggerated rules which cause women—more especially young and unmarried women—to utter sentiments and thoughts totally at variance with their real ones, and to fear to pursue that conduct which their own consciences tell them would be pure and noble, yet which the cold and heartless conventionalists forbid. Could this fearful system of falsehood and deception, disguised as it is under the garb of refinement and delicacy, both of which are spurious—could this have been intended? Is it right?"

" No," cried Maud, " falsehood and hypocrisy, no matter how beautifully clothed, never can be right. As I said before, there are certain rules that are necessary, which, when prompted by good taste and good feeling, every man and woman of delicacy and refinement will respect."

" Not the slightest doubt of it; but the overstrained and exaggerated way with which society frames its regulations is vulgar, hypocritical and altogether disgusting."

" I rejoice to hear you say so," said Maud, " and am glad that one at least, can attribute my freeness and independence of opinion to the right motive, and know it is not want of delicacy that prompts it, but a knowledge of the paltry value, nay, the injurious influence, of that system society dictates, of restraining all the noblest sentiments, the kindest sympathies of the heart."

For a few minutes there was silence. They both raised their eyes to look at the brightly shining moon. Then Maud spoke,

"Sir Harry and I were speaking to-day of the sons of families in poor circumstances, we more especially alluded to those of gentle birth and breeding, though poor in worldly wealth, that class, that, by the proud, money-getting merchant, is so despised, the class of poor gentry. How often do we see a family of this description, the sons placed in professions, the parents striving and denying themselves every luxury, and, I may say, almost necessaries, to educate them for those professions, and yet there are two or three daughters residing at home, a burden upon their parents, though they, in their affection, will not admit it to be so. Can these be supported for nothing? Are there not food and clothing and other expenses that must be incurred? Yet they never dream of the selfish conduct they are pursuing in living thus in idleness, making no effort to relieve their parents of the burden of their maintenance, even for a time. Why should they not make their effort? Because, forsooth, it is contrary to the customs of society. Is it not lamentable to see what unconscious slaves even people possessing a moderate share of sense become?"

"The great cause of that erroneous usage of which you speak, my dear Maud," replied Augustus, "is neither more nor less than a feeling of false and paltry pride which exists in every narrow mind. Self-deceivers are, I believe, the largest class in the world; even those who really know themselves the best deceive themselves in some way. It is human nature so to do. But, apropos to what you and my brother were talking over, I quite agree with you that it is unjust when the girls of a family do not make themselves useful as well as the male portion. But you must remember the world will look down upon them as being very poor and obliged to send their girls into remunerating situations, and fear of the world's contempt is far stronger than prudence or the promptings of common sense; then there are so few ways in which a woman can earn a livelihood. I mean a woman of education. I know but of two, the situations of governess or companion. In too many cases these places are wretched drudgery."

"Is it more drudgery than the early uphill years of a young curate, a young surgeon, or lawyer, or a lieutenant in the army or navy, who have nothing beyond their pay to live on? Oh! no, Augustus, it must be a mean and grovelling mind that could contentedly sit down in idleness, while her brother is working hard. Why should the daughters alone not know and feel the disagreeables—the hardness of poverty. Why should they alone be idle. This is another of the absurd usages of society, which it would be more honourable and noble to break through than to adhere to."

"But it is not always the girl's fault that she

assists not her parents in their poverty. Before I judged, I would enquire first had she been properly brought up; for how many are there whose educations have been so neglected as to leave them incapable of entering upon any remunerative situation. It is too much the case with common minds to consider the teaching of girls but of little moment. Thus, while we see parents giving their sons classical educations— the very highest that can be bestowed upon them, their daughters get little beyond that plain, homely English instruction, which must be attained by all persons, but still far from sufficient to form the education of a gentlewoman, or for enabling her to obtain employment for gaining a livelihood suitable to her position. Is this right?"

"No, decidedly not," answered Maud.

"Was the education of women placed upon a higher footing and were their heads led to think on and study profounder subjects, and their hearts left to nature's guidance, unsullied and untrammelled by society's verdict, a purer, higher, better tone would pervade the whole civilised world; and one day, Heaven grant this may be."

"We shall not live to see that day," replied Maud.

"Perhaps not, but we must live in hope that a greater desire will be manifested throughout every class of society for advancement in knowledge."

"By-the-bye, Maud, do you intend publishing another book before you become my wife?" asked Augustus.

"Yes," she said, in a tone of unconscious sadness, "I am engaged on my last work."

"Not your last, my dear Maud," said Augustus, somewhat startled by the solemnity of her manner.

"My last before I leave England," replied his companion, with a peculiar passing smile, for the expression of sadness had again settled on her face.

"Well then, my love, my poem shall be published at the same time."

Maud looked at him, whilst a pleasurable

expression was on her countenance, which, however, was almost instantly replaced by one of sadness, for a mighty weight was at her heart, a dark foreshadowing of the future hovered over her young spirit.

They were retracing their steps homeward; the pure, pale moon glided swiftly on through the heavens, and the wind was rising, as it is wont to do in the autumn, suddenly, yet gently, causing the leaves to flutter distinctly in the breeze, and a low moaning sound was heard through the branches like the soft, melancholy note of the Æolian harp. There was a solemnity in the scene and in the hour, so still and quiet save the soughing of the wind. It was a night almost peculiar to the autumn season, a time that is apt to sadden the heart, the time of withering and decay; yet withal, perhaps, the loveliest in the whole year. They walked on without speaking, each deep in thought, Augustus revelling in the idea of future happiness in his married life with so intellectual and beautiful a woman, of travelling with her through lands of surpassing magnificence and beauty. Maud, on the contrary, was full of self-reproach for having promised to be his wife, having, in a moment of what she now deemed madness, forgotten her early and only love. Still her word was pledged, and however much she might suffer she was determined to make him as happy as she could, although her love she could not give him. She would not for the world that Augustus should know the void in her heart, but she fully made up her mind that she would not cast a gloom over his happiness.

On and on they walked, and a feeling of deep solemnity gradually came over them both as they approached the mansion where so many happy days had been spent, and which they were in a few hours going to leave for an indefinite number of months, perhaps ,years. Maud's imaginative mind fancied the moaning of the wind, as it sounded through the branches and scattered the leaves across the path, a warning of evil near at hand, to bid her beware how the peaceful hours were flitting away and to prepare for some unforseen misery.

At length Augustus broke the silence, the sound of his voice causing Maud to start.

"How mournfully the wind sounds to-night, yet it is beautiful. It seems like the music of angels singing us a farewell memory. Does it not, dear?"

"Yes," replied Maud, "it is beautifully solemn."

"Can you not discern music in it?"

"Yes," she returned, with a smile, "it is melancholy, but fitting music for our last night at this beautiful spot."

They reached the front of the mansion, but before entering they turned round to gaze once more on the beautiful landscape, as if reluctant to leave the spot.

## CHAPTER XII.

THE following morning before sunrise the carriage was at the door. It had been ordered thus early (the railway station being some miles distant) to enable the travellers to go by an early train, the distance to Bridgnorth being considerable. The morning was cold, and a thick haze hung over the dense wood and extensive park.

"I fear, Maud, the morning air is too cold for you?" said Lady Boothby, soon after they were seated in the carriage.

"It is rather chilly," Maud replied, as she moved forward to catch a last glimpse of the scene where she had spent so many hours and days of dreamy happiness.

"You seem to regret losing sight of the old trees," said Sir Harry, smiling.

"Indeed, I do. I don't know how it is, but I feel a presentiment that I shall never again gaze upon this gorgeous scenery," and Maud heaved a deep sigh.

"I trust, my dear," said Lady Boothby, "that you will spend many happy weeks and months here after you return from abroad."

"Yes," said Augustus, "and with better health to enjoy its beauties."

The carriage went at a rapid pace, and the travellers' attention was every now and then enlisted to admire the charming scenery through which they were passing.

At length the railway station was reached, and in a few minutes all the party were seated in a carriage, of which they were the sole occupants.

As the train reached Bridgnorth, Maud's anxiety became exceedingly great, and her lips lost all their colour.

Lady Boothby observed the change, and taking her friend's hand, said—

"Why, Maud, your hands are as cold as ice. It is not so very chilly, certainly not so cold as it was in the morning."

"I am very cold. I always suffer a good deal from the effects of the autumnal evenings."

"How so?" asked Augustus.

"I cannot tell," Maud replied.

The train entered the station. The gas was lighted, and Maud looked anxiously at the crowd on the platform. One amongst the number assembled there looked into every carriage. Maud instantly recognised the gentleman—it was her cousin, Cecil Woodhouse, but she made no remark; she felt an inward conviction that new trials awaited her.

The train stopped, and Sir Harry and his brother stepped from the carriage on to the platform. Maud saw Woodhouse coming towards them, and her feelings were almost uncontrollable. She felt she would have given much not to have introduced Cecil Woodhouse to her affianced husband just then. She purposely dropped her handkerchief as Lady Boothby followed Sir Harry, and bending down to search for it, obtained time to subdue her emotion.

Mr. Woodhouse was at the station by request of Mrs. Courtenay, much to his annoyance, for he was averse to meeting Maud with Mr. Boothby; but he was far too unselfish to let his own inclinations stand in the way of doing an act of kindness to Mrs. Courtenay.

Woodhouse had seen Sir Harry and his brother alight from the carriage, and felt certain from the *distingué* bearing of the former, and the equally aristocratic air of the latter, that they belonged to Maud's party.

Fixing his eyes upon Augustus, he mentally said—

"That man must be Maud's affianced—the gifted one who has won her young heart's love."

In another minute he saw the gentlemen assist the ladies from the carriage, and his suspicions were confirmed, for Lady Boothby, whom he knew, had taken her husband's arm, and Maud that of the gentleman, whom he now knew to be Mr. Boothby.

"Who is that gentleman coming towards us, Maud?" asked Augustus. "Do you know him?"

"Yes," answered Maud, looking in the direction Woodhouse was coming. "That is my cousin, Mr. Woodhouse. I suppose mamma thought it would be kind for some one to meet us."

"And so it is, exceedingly kind," said Augustus.

As Woodhouse approached within a few yards of them, Maud disengaging her hand from Mr. Boothby's arm, advanced to meet him. She held out her hand, and shook hands with her cousin warmly.

"How are you, Maud; I trust entirely recovered from the effects of your long illness."

"Yes, thank you; only a little weak. But let me introduce you to Sir Harry Boothby and his brother. With Lady Boothby you are already acquainted."

Greetings were exchanged, and Lady Boothby extended her hand, and shook that of Woodhouse's cordially.

Woodhouse and the travellers left the platform, and went through the station, on the outside of which a carriage was in waiting, and in less than half-an-hour they arrived at the gate of Mrs. Courtenay's cottage.

"What an exceedingly pretty place, Maud," said Augustus, as they walked up the garden path, "so pretty and so secluded."

"I am glad you like it," Maud replied.

Maud and Augustus were a little in advance of the rest, and when within a few yards of the house, Mrs. Courtenay was seen standing in the hall to give them welcome. Maud rushed forwards, and in a moment was folded in the arms of her mother.

Mr. Boothby had stopped, and from motives of delicacy, turned round to look after the rest of the party, so that the meeting between mother and daughter might be private.

"My precious darling!" Mrs. Courtenay exclaimed; "how very glad I am to see you again."

"My dear mother," said Maud, pressing her to her heart. "I, too, am equally delighted to be home once more."

Maud turned towards the door where Augustus was standing.

"Augustus," she said, "let me introduce you to my dear mother."

Mr. Boothby approached Mrs. Courtenay, who held out both her hands to welcome him, but for the moment was unable to speak. Augustus took the hands so kindly extended, and pressed them warmly, saying,

"This is a happy meeting I have often longed for. I am, indeed, delighted to be introduced to Maud's mother, of whom I have heard her speak with such devoted love."

Mrs. Courtenay's eyes filled with tears, as she pressed the hand of Augustus.

At this moment, Lady Boothby and Sir Harry came in, and after kissing Mrs. Courtenay affectionately, Lady Boothby introduced her husband, who was greeted warmly.

The ladies retired to their respective rooms to take off their bonnets, and ere they returned Woodhouse came into the dining-room.

"I am so much obliged to you, Cecil," said Mrs. Courtenay, "for seeing to everything for me."

Lady Boothby and Maud returned, and in a few minutes refreshments were served. Augustus and Woodhouse were seated next to each other, and for some time conversed, appearing mutually pleased. Maud was too fatigued to sit at the table, and she reclined upon a couch, her eyes involuntarily resting upon Augustus Boothby and Cecil Woodhouse. Oh! how painfully she felt, now that she was awakened to her true position, and to the full extent of her love for Woodhouse. Now it was that the whole force and intensity of her misery burst upon her. To be obliged to set a guard upon her every word and action—and what was worse, her every look, lest either should betray her love, a love that was deeply seated in her heart. Another sorrow was weighing her down, that she should be obliged to practise a deceptive part. In her own breast she felt the pledge she had given to Mr. Boothby had been spoken unconsciously, in an hour when the delirium of fever was stealing over her from excess of misery. At that moment how painfully the fact pressed upon her, that she was deceiving that high-souled man, whom she only respected—she loved another.

The agony of Maud's thoughts, as she lay gazing on the two men before her, caused a fearful sickness to oppress her, a choking sensation was in her throat, and her hands fell helplessly on the couch. She fainted. She remained in this state for a minute or two, until Lady Boothby turned round to address her, and, on seeing the ashy paleness of her face and lips, started up, and immediately perceived the cause.

"She has ainted," said Lady Boothby.

"Fainted!" exclaimed Mrs. Courtenay. "Oh! my dear child! the journey has been too long for her."

"Some water," cried Lady Boothby.

In an instant Cecil Woodhouse was by Maud's side, and picking up the handkerchief she had dropped, began wiping away the cold drops of perspiration that stood upon her forehead, and then taking her icy hands in his, clasped them tightly, to endeavour to communicate warmth. This occupied little more than a minute, and then seeing a slight tinge of colour return to Maud's pallid lips, he recollected himself instantly, and turning round, saw Mr. Boothby standing beside him, gazing on the prostrate form, his whole countenance betraying intense anxiety.

The colour mounted to Woodhouse's temples, and he instantly drew back. Why, he scarcely knew.

Augustus bent over the couch, whilst Mrs. Courtenay sprinkled Maud's face with water, and when she had partially recovered, Augustus raised her, and supported her in his arms, and Woodhouse noted the gaze of passionate love that shone in his eyes. After a minute or two, Maud opened her eyes and looked anxiously around.

"The journey has been too much for you, my love," said Mrs. Courtenay.

"Had you not better go to bed at once?" asked Lady Boothby; "the day has been a long trial for you, after your illness."

"I will go to your room with you, Julia," said Maud, languidly. "I am sure you must require rest."

"Yes, I shall be glad to retire, so take my arm."

Maud arose, kissed her mother, and shaking hands with Augustus, and Sir Harry, passed on to where Woodhouse was standing, and as she bade him good-night, he said—

"Good-night, Maud," in a low, almost tremulous voice, pressing her offered hand.

Their eyes met for a moment and were as quickly averted, and Maud and her friend left the room.

Woodhouse and Maud felt most painfully their position, and endured an intensity of misery that it is impossible to describe. They had deceived themselves and were now deceiving others.

\* \* \* \* \*

Let us now take a peep at Edith Ryan. For some time she had gone through her daily duties as she had ever done. Her father's comforts had been assiduously cared for; she had sang to him, read to him, and walked with him. She had done everything but talk to him. In spite, however, of all her loving kindness the poor old gentleman could not disguise from himself the fact that her health was failing, that her spirits were fearfully depressed, and that, from some cause, some recent trouble, some deep and firmly rooted sorrow. He knew grief was in her heart, but he had not the slightest idea of the cause, which was slowly but surely destroying his beloved child. He could no longer see her day by day becoming more fragile, and with tears in his eyes begged her to tell him if there was anything he could do to console and comfort her. Then the tears gathered in her eyes and the bright drops fell quickly.

"No, dear father," she cried, "you have seen rightly. I have affliction, misery, but you cannot lessen it—not all your precious, tender love can do that."

"Would not imparting the cause of your sorrow to me lessen it? Do you not know, my dear child, that I truly sympathise with you? Edith, my love, do not think I press you for your confidence. I know sorrow is sometimes too deep for words, so far down in the heart as never to be revealed even to a father's anxious eyes. But, my love, tell me one thing—has any man dared to deceive you?"

The old man's eyes flashed for a moment at the thought.

"No, dearest father, he never deceived me; it is I who have deceived myself."

Edith was not aware that in those few words she had revealed the nature of her sorrow, and she continued—

"I will tell you all, papa, for you have a right to my confidence, and there is none other on earth to whom I could lay open my heart. The facts are simply these: I mistook the acts of friendship for love, and when he spoke to me kindly, nay, I may almost say, affectionately, I thought he loved me, and gave him, unasked, my heart. It is only very recently I have found that I had deceived myself, and that his love is given to another, and to one more deserving."

"Not more deserving, my child; that were impossible," and tears came welling up into the father's eyes.

"Yes, papa, more fitting and more worthy of him. He has chosen one possessing a more brilliantly endowed mind, and an intellect which he, above all others can appreciate. He has chosen Maud Courtenay!"

"Maud Courtenay!" repeated her father; "and Augustus Boothby is the man who has caused all the anguish in your heart."

"Yes, dear father; but I alone am to blame."

"Oh! Edith, all that you have gained in leaving your father's home, is a broken heart."

"Promise me, dear papa, you will keep my secret locked up in your own breast. Do not tell even Ellen."

The promise was given and kept, and day by day, the old man did all in his power to console and soothe his daughter.

The day before Maud and her friends were expected at Bridgnorth, as General Ryan and his daughter were conversing on the subject, the former said—

"Edith, my love, now we are on the subject, it is better that I should know how to act. Most likely Maud will call here the day after she arrives, and it is more than probable she will bring Julia and the two gentlemen with her. Now, my love, if you do not wish it, you shall not see them. I can easily make excuses for you. At any rate you need only see Maud and Lady Boothby."

"No, dear papa," replied Edith, in a tremulous voice. "I think I can bear the trial, though a sad one I own it will be. At any rate I will meet him once, and then, if I feel that I am unable to endure the ordeal again I will see him no more. I shall not be here much longer."

"My child! my Edith! what can you mean?"

cried the father in an agonised tone. "Oh! merciful God! take not from me my treasure, my greatest comfort!" and the father's tears mingled with the daughter's.

It was decided that Edith and Augustus Boothby should meet. The poor girl felt that however great her suffering it would not be for long. Her deepest grief was the thought of leaving her father alone in his desolate home.

## CHAPTER XIII.

"WILL you call on General Ryan, and see how poor Edith is?" said Mrs. Courtenay to Maud, at the breakfast table.

"Yes," replied Maud.

"Perhaps you will go, too, Julia," continued Mrs. Courtenay; "they will be delighted to see you."

"Oh! certainly I will," replied Lady Boothby, "and shall be glad to introduce Sir Harry and Augustus to the General."

As she spoke the blood mounted to her forehead, as she wondered how Edith and her brother-in-law would meet.

About mid-day the whole party repaired to General Ryan's house. When they entered the drawing-room Edith was reclining on a couch, her father sitting by her side reading. Her hair fell in long curls each side her face, in which not a particle of colour was discernible; her eyes were closed, the long lashes resting on her pale cheek, contrasting distinctly with the colour of her hair, giving to her countenance a spiritual beauty rarely seen.

The visitors had entered the room before she mustered courage sufficient to open her eyes, and it was not till her father had risen and greeted them that she rose from the couch and feebly advanced. She embraced Maud affectionately, which embrace was as affectionately returned, the former seeing with regret how ill she was looking, but making no remark. Edith welcomed Lady Boothby and Sir Harry, and the last she held out her hand to was Augustus, who said, as he pressed her hand warmly—

"I am delighted to meet you again, Miss Ryan, but I fear you are not well; you are looking so pale."

"I am not quite well," replied Edith; "but

there is nothing of importance the matter with me."

The conversation became general in which, however, Edith took little share. She sat on the couch close to Maud, who talked to her for some time.

"My dear General," said Mrs. Courtenay, "you and Edith must come and dine with us early in next week, and we will arrange a walking party the same day."

"I fear you must excuse Edith," said the General. "She is far from well, and the night air would be injurious to her."

"Oh! she need not fear the night air; she shall stay with us. Maud will take charge of her."

"I hope Miss Ryan will be much better and stronger next week," said Augustus.

The General looked towards his daughter, who answered for him.

"I hope I shall be better, and if I feel strong enough the change will do me good."

The day was fixed for the dinner party, and

Mrs. Courtenay and her friends soon after took their leave, promising that some of them would call on the morrow to enquire after Edith's health.

"How dreadfully altered Edith is," exclaimed Maud, as soon as they were outside the house.

"Yes," said Mrs. Courtenay, "she is fearfully altered. I have been very anxious about her for some time. I have often talked to her father about her, but he says little on the subject. I cannot conceive what has caused her illness."

"How long has dear Edith been so unwell?" asked Lady Boothby, who, with a woman's shrewdness guessed the cause, and sighed as the thought flashed across her mind.

This was not the first time Lady Boothby had feared the result of her brother-in-law's engagement being made known to Edith would cause great pain to the poor girl; but she had no idea that her love for Augustus had been so deeply fixed. She kept her thoughts within her own breast, for she saw plainly the mischief was irreparable. Mr. Boothby expressed himself shocked at the great change that had come over Edith; but had no idea that it was he who had caused that change. He still thought her very lovely, and for a moment he called to mind the pleasant hours he had passed in her society in Portman Square, and even smiled when he thought how very much her beauty and innocence had induced him to believe he had loved her.

A week had passed away since the Boothbys had arrived at Bellevue Cottage, and the day fixed for the walking excursion and dinner party had arrived. Mr. Raymond and his wife had arrived at the General's, and Mrs. Gibson and Dora at Mrs. Courtenay's the preceding evening. About three o'clock the whole party, including Woodhouse, assembled at Bellevue Cottage; Edith was mounted on a quiet pony—her father walked by her side, taking the road to Fort Tower, which commanded the finest view in the neighbourhood, both seaward and inland. To reach this tower, the pedestrians had to walk through beautiful lanes, such as can only be seen in Devonshire; then they traversed the high-

road, and then again passed through lanes. It
was, truly, a lovely walk; but as often happens,
there were some in that assembly who could not
enjoy it. By chance, they were unfortunately
grouped; how the *contretemp* happened none
could tell. Maud and Woodhouse found themselves walking side by side. Augustus was on
one side of Edith's pony, and her father, who
never left her, was on the other, whilst Ellen
walked beside her father. Lady Boothby and
Dora paired together; Mrs. Gibson and Mr.
Raymond; Mrs. Courtenay and Sir Harry.

Maud and Cecil Woodhouse had met frequently
during the past week, and a wretchedness of a
whole lifetime had been concentrated in those
seven days. Their positions were too painful to
be understood by those who have never experienced the bitter trial. They conversed on all
kinds of subjects; but every now and then, in
spite of their endeavours to avoid it, an awkward
pause would ensue, embarrassing to both. The
long separation seemed, if possible, to have increased their love tenfold. There were times

when a feeling of desperation arose in Woodhouse's heart, when he thought he must tell her that he loved her, and her alone. It was strange, but patiently as he had suffered, nobly as he had striven to atone to Dora for the involuntary selfishness of conduct he had once been guilty of towards her, a feeling of desperation was rising up at last; he had suffered too long, and too intensely. There are times—even in the purest mind, the noblest heart—when for a little season duty is forgotten, and passionate inclination obtains the mastery. It may possibly never be revealed unless, in an evil hour circumstances arise to favour the disclosure; then duty, right, all are forgotten, and the being of noble heart and mind will do that for which, in calmer moments, he will despise himself, and probably never cease to regret.

Cecil Woodhouse was becoming desperate from excess of misery. Since Maud's return to Bridgnorth there had been times when he had entirely forgotten Dora Gibson, and thought only of Maud, whom he had so long and seriously loved.

They had walked about a mile, when on coming to a steep ascent, Woodhouse, noticing how pallid and tired his companion appeared, offered her his arm.

"Lean on me, Maud," he said, "rest on my arm, as you used to do, long ago."

A shudder passed over Maud's frame as she heard those words—they recalled that one bright spot in her memory—the week she had spent at Pentlow Hall—when she had fancied, nay, almost believed that Cecil loved her.

"Thank you, Cecil; I am only too glad of your assistance, for the steepness of the hill has wearied me."

They were in advance of the rest of the party when they reached the summit, and Maud turned round as if to wait for the loiterers to join them, feeling that her *tête-à-tête* was growing each minute more painful.

Woodhouse looked at her, and she could not help noticing the expression of intense misery on his countenance.

"Are you tired of me already, Maud?" he

asked, in a tone and manner unlike himself. "Well, we will wait till *he* comes."

"Who comes?" said Maud, not merely surprised, but astonished at her cousin's words and manner.

"Mr. Augustus Boothby, of course; he will join us in a minute," and Woodhouse turned away, so that Maud should not see his countenance. She, however, did see it, and also the painful expression stamped upon it, without having the slightest idea what had caused such a look of misery, and acting upon the impulse of the moment, she said—

"Cecil, give me your arm; I am not equal to this long walk, and am thankful for your assistance. Do not let us wait for the others. I care not for their company for awhile."

"What, Maud!" cried her companion, taking her hand, "not even for *his?*"

"Not at this moment," she replied," and then with an assumed gaiety, added, "it is not well to be always in each other's company, we may grow weary of ourselves." A light, wild laugh escaped her lips, and fell discordantly on Cecil's ear; she could scarcely tell why she lifted her eyes to her cousin's, and met his calm eyes resting on her with an expression in them that made her start and think—

"Is it possible that some lingering feeling of friendship remains in his heart for me!" and a joyous sensation thrilled through her frame; but it was only for a moment, the flash of light was gone, and her mind became more wretched than before. At length they reached their destination, and were speedily joined by the rest of the party.

The day was clear and fine, and enabled them to discern the inland country for miles around, as well as far out to sea, upon which a noble fleet of ships of war were floating. It was a glorious sight, and there were those amongst the party who could appreciate it as it deserved.

"Do you remember, Maud," said Woodhouse, "how often we used to walk up here before—"

"Yes—yes," she replied, hastily, interrupting him, "I remember. What a beautiful sight it is! Those noble ships of war, far away on the broad expanse of blue water, and those dear familiar hills I love so well. Oh! how I delight in gazing upon all around us," and her eyes sparkled, and for a moment pleasure lighted up her countenance.

Woodhouse gazed upon her with undisguised admiration, and in a low voice, said—

"You are as intense a lover of Nature as when we used to walk together long ago, over the hills and through the lanes of this beautiful neighbourhood; when you used to tell me that you had seen in dream-land scenes brighter and fairer than these. Do you remember this, Maud?"

An ashy paleness overspread the maiden's countenance, as she faintly replied—

"I do, indeed;" and she thought to herself, "Why does he recall those hours—those days of self-deception, when I loved without really knowing it. Why? Because he knows not the utter wretchedness of my heart, my deep-devoted love for him; and, consequently, he knows not the double misery he causes by recalling those times, as if they were not indelibly burnt upon my memory, defying all my endeavours to erase them."

For some moments Maud stood gazing upon the scene around her, completely absorbed in her own thoughts. At length her reverie was disturbed by the voice of Augustus, bringing back the remembrance that to him alone she belonged. Oh! the anguish of her heart at that moment. She felt that her sorrow was never ending, that it was constantly increasing.

As Mr. Boothby approached, Woodhouse turned away, for he knew the expression of his countenance at that moment was not what he would have another behold. He felt utterly miserable; but as Mr. Boothby took Maud's hand in his own, and addressed her, Cecil remembered that she was affianced to another. For the moment, too, he had completely forgotten his own engagement with Dora. Now, however, he roused himself, and was once more the calm, high-principled, and somewhat stern man where duty and honour was concerned.

The reign of passion, short as it had been, was

over. Woodhouse felt no jealousy towards his successful rival, and now that a sense of his own duty had returned, he looked upon Mr. Boothby with respect, for he knew his mind was far superior to the great bulk of his fellows. He was also well aware that the love he entertained for Maud was a mighty love, and he rejoiced. The liking of Woodhouse and Augustus Boothby was mutual, the latter saw in his new acquaintance a noble minded man, one with whom he could sympathise, and whose conversation afforded no ordinary pleasure.

When Mr. Boothby joined Maud and Woodhouse, he spoke rapturously of the beauty of the landscape, and the three entered into an animated and cheerful conversation, a cheerfulness assumed by two of the party, but by the third with a deep joy at his heart. After a short time Woodhouse withdrew and left Maud and her lover alone.

"I like your cousin extremely, Maud," said Augustus, "I do not wonder that you all seem so fond of him, I never saw a man whose countenance bore so clearly the stamp of a noble mind."

"He is indeed a noble-minded man," replied Maud, "and is deservedly liked by all who know him," as she spoke her lip quivered from the intensity of emotion, and she continued, for her feelings were wound up to a pitch that gave her strength to say anything at the moment; aye, to speak even of him to her affianced husband, "and Dora Gibson, to whom he is about to be united is truly deserving of him. She will make a fitting wife, so good and amiable, no bitterness is in her nature, no sorrow in her heart. No, that is filled with nothing but love for him."

There was something peculiarly pleasing to Augustus in hearing Maud speak so affectionately and so highly of those friends, and he said—

"There is something in Miss Gibson very fascinating both in her appearance and manner I like to look on her young face. She is very beautiful. Did you ever notice how her expression varies when she is speaking to Mr. Woodhouse. She must be very young, Maud; she looks scarcely more than fifteen, though there is an air of thought on her countenance belonging to maturer years."

"She is, within a year or two, the same age as myself, and I am in my twenty-first year, you know," replied Maud, and she added, smiling, " you are a connoisseur of fair faces, which of the two before us is the highest class of beauty ?" she spoke lightly so as to draw her companion's attention from the subject on which he was before speaking.

"You are alluding, of course, to Miss Ryan and Miss Gibson. I consider neither of them of a high class of beauty, at least not according to my idea of it. Miss Ryan's, however, is the highest; her beauty is divine, a loveliness that is rarely seen on earth; so *spirituelle* is it that it seems like some angel's face, but to me, there is a something wanting, something more precious than that *spirituelle* expression. There is no deep thought on her exquisitely formed brow, or in her beautiful blue eyes. In these there is a pensive sadness which is the chief charm of her face. There is no indication of a lofty intellect, no stamp of genius, and that, dear Maud, is what I love to behold above all else."

He spoke in a low, fond voice, and Maud could not mistake his meaning, although it was the first time he had—even in the most distant and delicate manner—made the slightest allusion to her personal appearance, for Mr. Boothby was far superior to that class of men who compliment women on their exterior charms; how much less would he have been guilty of so gross an outrage on delicacy and refinement to a woman of Maud's stamp. But in the compliment that had almost unconsciously escaped his lips there was something so refined that even Maud appreciated it; a compliment which sprung evidently from his heart.

The whole party began to descend the hill. Augustus and Maud walked home together and lingered somewhat behind the rest.

"What a pleasant little coterie you form in Bridgnorth," said Augustus, as they strolled on arm-in-arm. " How different to the fashionable circles in London where we meet hundreds of people and feel not the slightest interest in scarcely any of them. Here you know and are known to all, taking a lively interest in each other's pleasures and sorrows. The Ryans, whom you have known from childhood, and that kind-hearted, unselfish Woodhouse, a man all must like. The ladylike Mrs. Gibson whose every look beams with affection and kindness, and her charming daughter, whose coming marriage with your cousin must, I am sure, cause you much happiness. In fact, dear Maud, your coterie forms a complete circle of love. Never before have I been thrown into a society where I met so many truly interesting members; it must be that, added to their natural charms, true friendship dwells amongst you, and consequently there is no restraint, no cold and systematic rules, to check the natural outpourings of your hearts to each other, for all seem as one family, whose interests are in common and in which strife is never heard."

Maud made no reply, for she was in dreamland.

" But, Maud," Mr. Boothby continued, " I do not mean to say that because there is so much love for one another in your little circle true sympathy is there also. I can well understand, dear girl, that although you are loved by all about you, there is little sympathy, for they could not understand you, could not comprehend; your mother loves you ardently, I can plainly see, but she does not appreciate your intellect. The only person who I believe most likely to have understood you, would have been your cousin Woodhouse. Did you never speak to him as you have spoken to me, of course not so freely, but did you never let him have a glimpse of your inner thoughts and give him an idea of the real power of your mind? Mr. Woodhouse, is, I am sure, no ordinary man, and would, I think, have appreciated you."

" No," said Maud, the colour rising to her brow, " you forget how many years I knew my cousin before I was capable of putting forth the powers of my mind, and to have talked to Cecil about my talent would have been ill-judged. To a certain extent he did appreciate me, but I never laid bare my strange deep thoughts to any human being but yourself. You have a mind that can sympathise with me."

Here the conversation was broken off, those in advance coming to that part of their walk where the roads diverged. General Ryan and Mr. and Mrs. Raymond took that to the General's house, to dress for dinner, but Edith went on with the rest to Mrs. Courtenay's in order to save her fatigue. When the General left Edith's side, Maud immediately took his place and Augustus led her pony. Poor Edith! what a fearful position she was placed in, what a difficult task she had to perform; what little strength she had left was fearfully taxed to enable her to bear the trials and constant anguish which, apparently, seemed never ending. Her only consolation was, she felt, that a few weeks, nay, perhaps a few days would end all her trials, all her anxieties.

Maud noticed with affectionate solicitude Edith's fading appearance, and though she did not for a moment suspect the cause, felt certain there was some secret sorrow at her heart, some canker daily and hourly undermining and destroying her health. Maud's affection for Edith and her sister was that of a loving sister, but Edith had always been the one she had loved most tenderly.

"Are you very much fatigued, dear Edith?" asked Maud, as they stopped before the gate of her mother's cottage.

"No, I think I feel considerably invigorated by the refreshing air and the pleasant ride," she replied with that soft pensive smile, so peculiar to her.

Augustus lifted her from her saddle, and then drawing her arm through his own assisted her up the garden walk. A passing thought of other days crossed his mind; but it was only for a moment. He little imagined how those "other days" were robbing that young creature, leaning on his arm, of her very life. A warm blush stole over her pale cheek, her companion saw it, but guessed not its cause. Edith was conducted by Maud to her bedroom, to dress for dinner.

The two girls talked for a short time upon the passing events of the day, and Maud assisted Edith from time to time in her toilette, amusing her by some anecdote, or by some mention of Augustus Boothby's admiration of the scenery. It was in vain, however, that Maud tried to arouse her companion's spirits. Utter misery was stamped upon her features, and in a moment of unconsciousness she uttered words that startled her companion. Maud, however, was unlike her mother. She never sought another's confidence, considering it both unfeeling and indelicate to do so, but now that Edith's countenance betrayed the misery at her heart, she involuntarily asked her,

" My darling Edith, what is the cause of that look of unhappiness — that anguish on your countenance? Tell me, love, if there is anything I can do to alleviate it. I am sure some secret sorrow is wearing away your very life."

Edith's head sank upon her friend's bosom;

she was completely prostrate, unable to utter a word, or make a single effort to conceal her deep emotion, whilst a torrent of tears gushed forth and fell upon her pallid cheeks. For some time there was perfect silence, which neither seemed desirous of breaking; but at length Edith said, with a choking sensation in her throat—

"My dearest Maud, you cannot remove my sorrow, nor can you alleviate it; but, love, do not grieve for me. I feel assured that in a very few weeks, perhaps in a few hours, I shall be at rest, where sorrow and trouble is unknown."

Like a flash of lightning it was suggested to Maud's mind that Edith was dying, and a half-suppressed groan escaped her lips. And, however much she desired to do or say all she could to alleviate the sorrow-stricken girl, she seemed powerless to speak or to act. For some time not a word was uttered. At length, however, Edith roused and said,

" Dear Maud, will you arrange my hair for me. I feel too weak to do it myself."

"My dear Edith," said Maud, "I will do it with pleasure; but perhaps you would rather remain up-stairs than go to the drawing-room."

"No, thank you, I shall be better in a few minutes."

As she said this a slight shudder passed over her fragile frame, possibly from the recollection of the almost certain trial she would have again to encounter in beholding the man she loved exchanging impassioned glances with his affianced bride. This would have been a powerful trial even had she been in robust health, but now that her physical strength was fast failing, it was almost too much for poor human nature to bear.

Their toilettes completed, the two friends descended to the well-filled drawing-room, where they found Mrs. Raymond and her husband and General Ryan, who had a minute or two before arrived. The dinner passed off pleasantly enough to some, and apparently to all, for even those whose hearts were aching assumed a gaiety which none but themselves could detect. Little did any of them suspect how soon poor Edith would be taken from them, all thinking that a few weeks would restore her to health.

The gentlemen did not sit long when the ladies had retired to the drawing-room, and soon after the reunion Edith said to Maud, who was sitting beside her—

"I wish you would sing."

Augustus Boothby came up before Maud could reply, saying—

"Maud, my love, do sing us a song. We all want music to-night. Do we not, Miss Ryan?"

"I had only the moment before asked Maud to sing one of her own songs," replied Edith, with a sweet, heavenly smile, instantly followed by a look of intense agony as Augustus led Maud to the piano, and seated himself close by her side.

Maud sang song after song—now the impassioned music of Italy that breathes love in every note, now the exquisite melodies of Tom Moore, with an expression and pathos that none but himself could ever have given. At length she ceased. Perfect silence reigned throughout the room; the fall of a pin might have been heard, so entranced had been all her listeners. Augustus led her from the piano, and pressing her hand spoke some fond words in appreciation of the exquisite music she had given. He took her to the seat next to Edith, and after a few words of thanks from the invalid, he said—

"Miss Ryan, do you feel well enough to sing to-night. You used to sing some of our English ballads charmingly."

A flush of crimson instantly overspread the poor girl's face and neck, and for a moment or two, she was powerless to reply, for Mr. Boothby's remark had recalled a time when she fondly hoped and believed all was bright before her; when she thought she might indulge in " young love's dream," and that it never could be dispelled. But what a change had come " o'er the spirit of her dream!" A shudder passed over her as she replied—

"Thank you, Mr. Boothby, I am much too weak to sing to-night."

Augustus, struck by the tone, gazed earnestly into her face. Just at the moment Edith raised her eyes, and saw those of Augustus looking enquiringly at her, with an expression of mingled admiration and grief. She took one glance at his handsome face, then her head dropped lower and lower, till it rested on her bosom, and her luxuriant hair fell over her face, like a veil.

Maud witnessed the whole scene, and a feeling, such as she could neither comprehend nor define came over her, and, like a flash of lightning, a new light seemed dawning upon her. "Did Edith love Mr. Boothby? Had Mr. Boothby ever loved Edith?" These were questions which floated across her brain. She took no notice nor made any remark, but she determined to watch.

Mr. Boothby looked on Edith with sorrow, for he plainly saw there was misery in that one glance she turned upon him ere her head drooped; but not the slightest idea of the truth occurred to him that he, and he alone, had been the cause of the fading of that delicate flower.

Woodhouse and Sir Harry had been engaged speaking of authors, both ancient and modern. The former was anxious to hear the baronet's opinion on ambition, a subject on which Sir Harry spoke and felt warmly, and he said—

"There are those, undoubtedly, who write for money; but these are only a grovelling few. The larger part of authors write involuntarily, as it were; they write because they cannot help it, and to these praise or blame has no effect; they work for the good of their fellow creatures, and with the noble wish to put forth that genius with which God has blessed them, but from no paltry pride. Look, for instance at my brother and Miss Courtenay, they care not one jot for the world's praise —they seek only the commendation of One. Do you think they would have been content to live in indolence, keeping this noble gift to themselves? No, such selfishness is not in their nature. Though they find a use and a beauty in every atom of creation, would they have been content to live in retirement and luxury? I am sure they would not."

" I most cordially agree with you, Sir Harry, in all the sentiments you have uttered, and—"

Woodhouse's reply was interrupted by the approach of General Ryan and the Raymonds.

" Good night, Woodhouse; we are going, for it is getting very late. You stay here for the night, I suppose?" said the general.

" No," replied Woodhouse, " the house is well filled already."

" Well, then, come and sleep at my house, instead of taking that long walk to Pentlow Hall."

"If it will not put you to inconvenience, I shall have much pleasure in accepting your kind offer," said Woodhouse, and after saying good-night to Mrs. Courtenay and her friends he left with the General.

Previously to retiring for the night, Augustus was talking to Edith, when Maud came to accompany her to her room.

"Good-night, Miss Ryan," said Augustus. "I trust you will be better and stronger to-morrow. We will take another ride; I think the one you had to-day refreshed you. Good-night," and he affectionately pressed her hand for a minute in his own.

The action, and the words which he spoke, and the manner in which he uttered them, were suggested by pure motives of kindness, and a certain feeling, perhaps, of sympathy, for he saw that she was languid and ill, but he suspected not the extent of misery that at times racked her young heart. The kind words which he uttered and the pressure of her hand sank deep into her heart.

"Here is another and stronger proof, that friendship was all he ever felt for me," she murmured.

How the poor invalid managed to go through the sad ordeal of leave taking she knew not, but she restrained her feelings till she reached Maud's room, and the moment she entered she threw herself into a chair and wept bitterly. Her strength gave way, for the friend of her childhood was not a restraint powerful enough to cause her to make another effort. Edith, at all times, no matter whether friends or strangers were present, had the greatest difficulty to restrain or conceal her emotions, and now that she was alone with Maud, all the trifling fortitude which she possessed, left her, and a deep, agonising groan escaped her lips.

Maud's suspicion that Edith loved Augustus Boothby was almost confirmed by this sudden and violent grief so immediately after parting with him; Maud had watched her young friend, and saw her countenance flush, when Augustus spoke kindly, nay, almost affectionately to her whilst bidding her good-night.

" Oh, God !" mentally soliloquised Maud, ".is another sorrow to be added to my already overburthened heart?" but with a powerful effort she put aside her own grief and endeavoured to assuage that of her poor suffering friend. Gently and soothingly she laid the weary head upon her shoulder, without speaking a word, for she was too well versed in such extremities not to know that the sympathy of silence was the most acceptable and the most delicate of all, especially in grief such as that before her. Gradually the weeping girl grew calmer, once more that angelic face was raised, and when she looked up into Maud's eyes, the passionate emotion had passed.

"Dearest Maud," she cried, "you know not how comforting your more than sisterly kindness is to me; you will be rewarded for it. I feel so very weak and ill to-night that I must ask you to help me in undressing. I shall not be a trouble much longer; I feel the end is near at hand."

"Oh! Edith, my love," cried Maud, the bright tears filling her eyes, "say not so. Is there no tie here on earth? Your poor father—nay, all of us. You know how sincerely we all love you."

"Yes," replied the invalid; "I know you do, but—" and she paused.

"But what, Edith?" asked Maud. "Can nothing be done to alleviate your sorrow? Is there anything I can do to remove the grief that is, I am sure, destroying you?"

A shudder convulsed Edith's frame, as she replied—

"No, dear Maud, to you I could not even name it. Will you assist me in undressing—I am very weary."

Hour after hour sped on, still neither of the friends slept ; they did not speak, each fearing to disturb the other. Maud lay so still that Edith thought she was asleep, and many heartrending sighs fell upon her companion's ear, during the stillness of night. At length, however, Maud knew by the gentle breathing that Edith slept. Yes, sleep came at last to the worn out mind and body

Presently Maud heard a muttering, but at first she could make out nothing distinctly ; Edith was dreaming and talking in her sleep. Maud listened attentively, fancying she had caught the name of Augustus. At length she heard her murmur—

"He never deceived me—I deceived myself. To-night he called me 'Edith,' as he used to do. Dear Augustus!"

Then the sleeper ceased, and in a minute or two again breathed softly and gently.

Maud was convinced that her suspicions were correct, and she lay deeply pondering over the way in which she should act; she felt a certainty in her own mind that the man she had believed to be so high-minded, so honourable in everything, must have sought to win her poor friend's love. The result of her cogitation ended in her forming a resolution that she determined at the proper time to carry out. Misery seemed rushing in upon her with redoubled force.

She sat up in the bed, and put her face in her hands, but, unlike the sleeper beside her, she shed not a single tear, although her sorrow was quite as intense. Maud closed not her eyes again that night, and gladly welcomed the daylight; she was up and nearly dressed before her companion, whose physical weakness caused her to sleep long and soundly awoke.

"Do not get up, dear Edith," said Maud; "you had better have your breakfast brought up to you."

"Thank you, Maud," replied Edith. "I fear it will cause trouble."

"Not in the least; I will bring the tray myself. You are not strong enough to rise so early in the morning."

"Thank you, dear. I shall be very glad to indulge a little longer; I feel very weak."

It was with strange feelings that Maud met her affianced husband that morning; a fear was on her mind now, though she scarcely *dared* to acknowledge it—one that a few days before she would have scorned as having the slightest connection with the man she had held in such high estimation. Unconsciously to herself there was considerable restraint in her manner towards him, and even more than usual earnestness; and several times her eyes were fixed on him scrutinizingly, yet mournfully.

After breakfast Maud asked Lady Boothby if she were disengaged.

"Quite, my love," Lady Boothby replied. "Why do you ask?"

"I wish to have half an hour's conversation with you."

"I shall be very pleased to have half an hour's chat with you."

"Suppose we go to your room. We shall not be likely to have any interruption there. Edith is in mine."

"Poor girl! she is, I fear, seriously ill," said her ladyship.

Maud and her friend left the breakfast room, and in a couple of minutes were seated in Lady Boothby's bedroom. The former entered at once upon the subject that was on her mind.

"Julia," she said, "I am about to ask you a plain question—one I am certain you will answer me truthfully, for, as you will at once see, it is of great importance not only as regards myself, but others who are not here—of vast importance to those to whom both you and I are fondly attached."

"I do not know what your question may be, dear girl, but you may rely upon my answering it truthfully."

"Did Augustus," asked Maud, with considerable emotion, " ever seek to win the love of Edith Ryan?"

Lady Boothby's face flushed crimson, and her eyes were averted from the searching, scrutinizing, earnest gaze fixed upon her.

" Maud," she began, " it is not fair—"

Maud stopped her abruptly, and with considerable sternness, said—

" Julia, there must be no concealment—no subterfuge. I must hear the truth, let that truth be what it may."

" What has induced you to ask me such a question?"

" Because I have discerned that Edith loves your brother-in-law. And—and—"

" And what?"

" That—if you will know it—that the unrequited love is destroying the poor fragile child."

" Poor Edith!"

" Now, Julia, tell me—did Augustus seek her love?"

" Is it right that I should answer the question?"

"I see no reason why you should not. If you will not, I have no alternative but to apply to Augustus; and he, I am sure, is far too proud to excuse himself by any subterfuge, if he has been wrong, or to palliate conduct which he now must feel was both cruel and unmanly."

Lady Boothby felt that there was no escape, so she deemed it better to reply, for she plainly discovered that if she did not her brother-in-law would lie under a suspicion of a heavier charge than he altogether deserved.

"I must confess, at one time, I thought Augustus loved Edith. Once I taxed him with my suspicions, and asked if he intended proposing to her."

"Did he acknowledge it?"

"No. He admitted that he thought very highly of her. To use his own words, as far as I can remember, he said, 'Edith is of too simple a nature—too unsoaring a mind to make me happy as a wife.' That he paid her great attention during her visit to me last year, I must candidly admit, but I feel assured he never told

Edith he loved her, or made her an offer of marriage."

"The truth of what you say, I know from Edith's own words; but I also know from her that he must have paid her devoted attention. I am obliged to you, Julia, for your information," she continued, in a grave manner, with a calm voice. "I now know how to act."

"What would you do?" said Lady Boothby, greatly agitated. "Poor Augustus! What will become of him? Maud, think calmly before you decide. Have mercy on him."

"I will," returned Maud, gravely; "and on Edith, too."

Maud left the room without another word, leaving Lady Boothby trembling with fear for the fate of the brother-in-law who was so dear to her.

## CHAPTER XIV.

WHILST Maud and Lady Boothby were conversing in the latter's bed-room, Edith had dressed herself, and gone down into the drawing-room, where she found Mrs. Courtenay, who was greatly alarmed at the change that had come over the poor girl's countenance, and which the excessive weakness she exhibited whilst her old friend laid her upon a couch made more evident. Mrs. Courtenay determined on sending for General Ryan without delay.

Lady Boothby did not leave her bed-room till sometime after the conversation she had had with Maud, and Mrs. Gibson, and her daughter, and Sir Harry Boothby were out; so Edith and Mrs. Courtenay were the only occupants of the drawing-room, and as the former closed her eyes, the latter kept silence, going on with some fancy needle-work.

Maud, when she so suddenly left Lady Boothby, went downstairs with a firm, quick step towards the dining-room, which she had seen Mr. Boothby enter not long before. Her hand trembled as she laid hold of the lock; it was, however, only for an instant, for her calmness returned, as she entered the room. No sternness was visible on her countenance, but a deeper sadness than usual was depicted there, although mingled with it there was great firmness and a fixed determination.

Mr. Boothby was lounging in an easy chair, reading, but the moment Maud entered, he put down his book and rose to meet her.

" My dearest," he said, taking her hand, "I have scarcely had an opportunity of speaking to you to-day. At breakfast you appeared more than usually thoughtful, you scarcely spoke, and immediately the meal was finished you vanished with my sister-in-law." Looking into her face he started. " My dear love, what is the matter with you? What has happened? Why, you positively look coldly on me."

Maud raised her eyes to his, looking earnestly and gravely; and, for a moment, a happy smile flitted across her countenance, as she thought—

"No, no; he cannot have been so cruel. His every look, and his high, broad, noble brow, speaks of nothing but truth and honour. Surely —surely I cannot have been mistaken in him."

At that moment Lady Boothby's words recurred to her, the recollection of the task she had imposed upon herself, and that a life was fast ebbing away beneath that roof subdued all other feelings. She still held her affianced husband's hand in hers, and leading him to the sofa, said gravely and kindly, if not affectionately—

"I do not look coldly on you, Augustus, but the subject which brought me here is one of the greatest importance, not only to us but to another. May I entreat you, therefore, to listen to me attentively and patiently."

"Most assuredly I will, my love," said her companion.

"Augustus, when Edith Ryan was on a visit to your brother's house the season before last, were you not fascinated by her beauty, not only of person, but character."

"Most assuredly I was."

"Did you not learn to love her—and above all, did you not seek in every way to win her affection."

The poet turned pale as marble as his affianced wife spoke these words, and the whole truth, for the first time, flashed like lightning across his mind, as with a voice of exceeding agony he cried—

"Great Heaven! Have I done this wrong? Then God be merciful unto me, for I committed it unintentionally—yes, Maud, without knowing it. Listen to me. When I first saw Edith Ryan, my heart was ill at ease, and I was longing for some purer, brighter, rarer being to commune with—than those frivolous women of fashion by whom I was surrounded. From them I turned with disgust, and my spirit was both lonely and sad. At that period the angelic face of Edith appeared before me, and though I quickly saw that hers was not a nature to understand or sympathise with mine, I turned to the study of her sweet, innocent—nay, beautiful character, with delight. I learnt to regard her as a precious friend, and there may have been moments when I was lost in the intensity of my admiration for her heavenly countenance—and far more, her exquisite purity and beauty of mind, when I believed that I well-nigh loved her. But these moments were but fleeting. The sensation I experienced at that period was like that in a dream, it vanished when thought re-assumed its sovereign power. Then I knew I did not love her; there was a something wanting which all her beauty of face and her equally guileless character did not supply—that jewel I had sought in vain through life. Still, however, I regarded her as a dear and valued friend, and unconsciously—yes, Maud, I say it truthfully—unconsciously my manner assumed towards her a tone of affection, almost of fondness; and I loved to draw forth the innocent and beautiful ideas of her mind, which, though there was no greatness, no sublimity, was truly lovely.

"It was one evening, if my memory does not fail me, the last before Edith left my brother's house, that I spent with her alone. I saw I was not wholly indifferent to her; but, great God! I never for a moment dreamed or even guessed she loved me as you say she does. Perhaps then a faint fear arose that unconsciously I had induced her to regard me with too deep an affection; but that idea was almost instantaneously dispelled, all the bitterness of my nature caused chiefly by that festering wound I had received in my early youth, resumed its sway, and my trust in woman was shaken, till I met one whose every thought, whose inmost soul I trusted, above all others I had ever known; and in her alone I found that true gem—sympathy.

"Turn not away, dearest Maud; I will speak no more of yourself, but of that poor girl who unconsciously I have so deeply injured. Yes, but I knew it not. I believed that if she cared for me at all it was little more than a passing fancy. Maud, had I never been deceived or seen so much deception going on around me, I never could have mistrusted that pure truthful creature. Not that I believed her capable of deception—no, assuredly not; but my confidence had been shaken, and my heart was full of bitterness.

"Well, that last evening on which I was alone with her, I talked to her long and perchance in too tender a strain. When I bade her farewell a bright tear trembled in her eye. For the moment the sight of that tear softened my bitterness of spirit, and I thought, 'Surely there is one heart cares for me.' We parted, and though I often thought of her, and always with great interest, and, I may say, affection of no common degree, the soothing influence of her presence soon passed away, and all our friendly intercourse appeared like some pleasant dream that was past —faded away for ever.

"But, Maud, I solemnly assure you I did not,

knowingly or intentionally, seek poor Edith's love; had I known she loved me so deeply I would have asked her to be my wife and married her, even though my own life's happiness had been utterly wrecked. Maud, my treasure, do you not believe me?"

" Believe you?" cried Maud, proudly, as she gazed on the noble countenance now turned to her with a look of intense earnestness. "Yes, Augustus, I believe every word you have uttered to be truth, and I can completely understand your feelings. Well I can imagine how you were charmed and fascinated by Edith's beauty and innocence, by her freshness and purity of heart. Well, too, can I fancy your unconsciously assuming towards her a manner which she, poor girl, mistook for love. Edith Ryan is one of those ethereal rare beings, calculated to inspire in any heart something more nearly approaching love than friendship, or perhaps, I should say, a something softer, more tender mingled with the sentiment of friendship. Yes, Augustus, most truly do I believe you. I could not for a moment think that you sought to win her love, and having won it cast it ruthlessly away. I almost felt sure it could not be so.

"Now, for the saddest part of my tale," her voice trembled for a minute, but only for a minute, as she roused herself and proceeded to speak calmly. "Augustus, you must do my bidding; you must go to that suffering, nay, I fear dying young creature, and tell her you meant not to deceive her. Ask her—"

Mr. Boothby's face was not merely pale as marble, but it wore an expression of the deepest agony, and clasping his hands, ere Maud could complete the sentence, cried—

"Maud, I know what you would say, but I cannot do it. I never can. You wish me to ask Edith to become my wife. However much I wish to atone to her for the wrong I have unintentionally done, I cannot do that."

"No, Augustus, you mistake my intentions," Maud replied. "I wish not for that, even had it been possible, I know Edith too well to think that, knowing as she does, you love another she would for a moment listen to such a proposal. But, Augustus, are you aware that poor Edith is dying? I feel almost convinced, and so does she, that her days, if not her hours, are numbered."

"Oh, God! and am I her murderer? May Heaven have mercy on me."

He buried his face in his hands, and groaned in very misery.

Maud's heart was rent with pity as she beheld the utter prostration of her companion. She felt that she must endeavour to alleviate the agonising pain of the wound she had necessarily inflicted, and throwing her arm round his neck, and taking his cold, white hand in hers, said, soothingly—

"Dear Augustus, do not look upon yourself in that light. You won the love of Edith unconsciously; and oh! if ever mortal man had ample cause for distrust in woman, you had, and though it may seem unjust to those who know not the human heart, there are those, and I am one, who understand that an impression once formed is hard to be effaced, more especially where it has been burnt in upon the heart with a stamp so indelible as was that on yours. Besides, you guessed not even then, that poor Edith loved you; so, my dear Augustus, blame not yourself so severely, great sorrow you must feel."

"Maud, let no one call you harsh or unbending after this. You are the guiding star of my life. Sad would have been my lot, and doubly so now, had you not been near. You who can understand my heart and read my every thought. But—but Edith."

"Yes, of her let me speak," replied Maud. "Go to her, Augustus, and soothe her dying hours. Tell her it is no sin to rest her aching head upon your bosom. Tell her you will cherish her as a dear and precious friend. Let her know, if she does not already know it, that you meant not to deceive her, and let her feel that she is dear to you, that you value and prize her. Augustus, my love, it will soothe her dying hour to know that even though you love her not, you regard her with affection—the affection of an elder brother. Come, Augustus, come to poor Edith, for she is, I fear, dying."

Maud took his hand and led him towards the drawing-room. A sweet quiet pervaded the house. Edith was alone in the room, for Mrs. Courtenay had crept quietly away, and the rest of the party had gone out, thinking that the young girl slept. The room was partially darkened, and the day being a dull one increased the shadows that rested on the reclining form of the sleeper. There she lay like a broken lily, its beauty crushed by a blast too rude and bleak, and now fading gradually away. Her eyes were closed, and the approach of Maud and Augustus was so gentle that she heard them not. They observed that her lips moved and her hands were clasped in prayer. As she drew nearer to her Redeemer her thoughts became less tainted with earthly things, and she prayed in hope and confidence for that rest to which she had so long looked forward.

At length Edith's lips ceased moving, and in a minute or two after Maud pronounced her name.

When she unclosed her eyes and beheld Augustus Boothby and Maud standing beside her she gave a sudden start, but uttered not a word.

Mr. Boothby saw at a glance how sadly changed she had become since the previous evening, and scarcely knowing what he did he swiftly but gently sank down upon his knees beside her, and taking one of the small emaciated hands in his said—

"Edith—Edith! forgive me the mighty wrong I have done you. This is no time for concealment and false delicacy. I won your love long ago without knowing it. I thought your affection for me was but a passing fancy of your young heart which would soon be obliterated. I now come to ask and crave forgiveness, and to tell you, dear Edith, that I love and treasure you as a brother, as a valued friend; and should it please our Heavenly Father that you be spared to me I will endeavour to prove it to you by a life devoted to securing your peace and happiness. Believe me it is not mere words that I speak; how deeply, how bitterly, I regret the conduct which has appeared so cruel and unmanly, but which, Edith, I solemnly assure you was not intended as such. Believe me, and oh! tell me that you forgive me."

Edith's little strength was all gone, the scene, short as it had been, had fearfully agitated her. She gave one glance at Maud, who stood beside her, and whom Augustus had begged to remain, and then a thrill of ecstasy ran through her frame. Her thin white arms were clasped round Mr. Boothby's neck, and the long masses of golden hair fell over his bowed head as a veil, and mingled with his dark locks.

"Augustus," she said in a scarcely audible voice, so fearfully weak was she, "there is nothing to forgive, and even if there had been the joy, the happiness of this moment would have swept all wrong from my remembrance. To die with you and dear Maud by my side is more than I expected, more than I could possibly have hoped for. Oh! beloved ones, the hour is drawing near. I feel that it is at hand. May God in His infinite mercy bless you both."

Her beautiful head rested on Mr. Boothby's

bosom, and his lips were pressed to her marble brow, as she breathed her last fond sigh. She lay thus, gently, peacefully a little while, and then they knew that she was dead. A loving smile rested on her face which seemed as a light sent down from Heaven, and the small white hands still lay within the poet's clasp, as they had been in life. Oh! what a sweet, calm, happy death was hers.

## CHAPTER XV.

Poor Edith Ryan's body was removed to Maud's bed, and both Maud and Augustus mourned over her bitterly; the latter with feelings no pen can express. For some time neither felt disposed to disturb the solemn silence around them. At length, however, Maud said in a low, sad voice—

"Augustus another sad task devolves upon me, I must go at once and break the painful fact of poor Edith's death to my most valued and dear old friend, General Ryan."

Mr. Boothby was speechless, his heart was filled with the deepest sorrow; now it was that the whole force of his imprudence rushed upon his mind.

Maud continued—

"Augustus, how sad it is to see such heavenly beauty, snatched at so early a period of life from earth. But thank Heaven! she is beyond the reach of mourning and of grief. Her poor father, he to whom she was the light and joy of existence; how can he be consoled for or reconciled to so fearful a calamity."

"Maud, Maud, what can I say; what can I do to soften the misery he will endure when he learns that the child he so passionately and so affectionately loved, has gone from him for ever, as far as this world is concerned."

Maud left the room, leaving Augustus, who was on his knees in prayer, and descended to the dining-room, requesting her mother not to go into the bed-room, or allow anyone else to do so.

"Why not, my love?" asked Mrs. Courtenay, astonished at the request.

"Because," replied her daughter, "there is one there who wishes to be alone with the dead."

Mrs. Courtenay said no more; she believed

that her good and worthy friend, the General, was the one alluded to, and that he had come to the house without her knowing it.

As she left the room, Maud saw the General and the Raymonds, accompanied by Cecil Woodhouse coming towards the house, and she instantly went to meet them, while Mrs. Courtenay remained in the dining-room.

"How is my darling Edith?" was the first question of the poor General, asked in a most anxious tone.

Maud slipped her little cold white hand into his and motioning the others not to follow, led her valued friend into the drawing-room which was vacant.

"Maud, my love," said the poor father, "there is something you fear to tell me. My child! my Edith. Is she—is she—oh! merciful Heaven! she is not dead!" and the distracted father looked searchingly and wildly, in his companion's face.

Maud saw instantly that he suspected the worst, and after a moment's consideration deemed it most advisable to tell him the sad, melancholy truth.

"Poor Edith has indeed left us, dear General Ryan; gone to a brighter, happier home. It is for us who are left to mourn—not for her—not for her, but for ourselves— for the loss we have sustained. We must remember that she is now in Heaven, among the pure and just. Oh! General, her last moments were as peaceful and holy as it is possible to imagine. Yes, a holy happiness was permitted her, which erased from her memory the misery she had so long suffered."

The father bowed his head in humble subjection to the Divine will, and wiping the tears, which were flowing plentifully down his cheeks, said—

"Maud, my love, take me to where she lies, so that I may look upon her precious face."

Maud led the grief-stricken man to the room where his child's corpse lay. The shadows of evening were fast spreading over the earth, and a dim solemn light pervaded the room where the Angel of Death had visited.

Had the poet in his lonely vigil thought of the lines penned years before by a greater poet than himself—

> " He who hath bent him o'er the dead,
> Ere the first day of death is fled;
> The first dark day of nothingness,
> The last of danger and distress;
> (Before Decay's effacing fingers
> Have swept the lines where beauty lingers),
> And mark'd the mild angelic air—
> The rapture of repose that's there—
> The fixed yet tender traits that streak
> The languor of the placid cheek,
> And—but for that sad shrouded age,
>    That fires not—wins not—weeps not—now—
>    And but for that chill changeless brow,
> Where cold obstruction's apathy
> Appals the gazing mourner's heart,
> As if to him it could impart
> The doom he dreads, yet dwells upon—
> Yes—but for these and these alone,
> Some moments—aye—one treacherous hour,
> He still might doubt the tyrant's power,
> So fair—so calm—so softly seal'd
> The first—last look—by death reveal'd."

The General leaned on Maud's arm, but as he entered the room he started and became fearfully agitated, as he caught sight of a man kneeling beside the bed on which the body of his loved child lay. Maud stopped, for a low, soft murmur issued from the lips of the kneeler. Humbly and earnestly the poet prayed, his head bent down and his hands clasped.

General Ryan looked at Maud, as if for explanation, but she placed her finger on her lip, and advanced towards Mr. Boothby.

"Augustus," she whispered, as she placed her hand gently upon his shoulder; "her father is here. Let us leave him for a while."

Mr. Boothby arose and turning round, beheld the sorrow-stricken father. He earnestly and sorrowfully pressed the old man's hand, and without a word being uttered by either of them, quietly left the room. They had not closed the door, when the grief-stricken voice of the father was heard—

"My child! my loved child, and are you gone from me for ever; my comfort, my only joy. Oh! why were you taken from me. Why was your young life blighted?"

As these heart-rending words fell upon the ear of Maud and her companion, she whispered—

"Go into the breakfast-room, Augustus. I will remain here for a time and then join you."

Augustus left her, and she gently shut the bedroom door, as the aged man put his arms round the dead body of his child; tears gushed forth and rolled down his cheeks, and his head rested on the marble hands of his idolised Edith. Maud stern, cold, as many, nay most believed her, was touched to her very heart's core, for there was in the sorrow before her no bitterness; the mourning of a father for a loved child, gone from his presence for ever on earth. Maud knew that sorrow would ere long be changed into joy, subdued and pensive it is true, but still joy; joy for the blessed knowledge and certainty that the tenderly loved one was gone to a brighter home, a resting place eternal.

The first hours of bitter anguish are selfish; but the noblest and best of God's creatures are not exempt from them—it is not in human nature that they should be. Maud's tears fell fast, and as she shaded her pallid face with her hands, her slight frame trembled from excess of emotion; she was about to turn from the room, and leave the afflicted father alone for awhile, to indulge in his sorrow, when the poor sufferer, raising his head at the moment, prevented her.

"Maud, my love," he said, in a low tone, scarcely above a whisper, so weak was his voice. "Maud, my love, do not go away; come here close beside me. You are sorrowing as I am for one we both loved so tenderly. Come near to me. The sympathy of your heart is dear to me, our sorrow is in common."

Maud glided quietly to her old friend's side, and knelt with him beside the form of her whose spirit had soared above. Long they knelt, and heartfelt prayers fell from the lips of both. At length Maud arose, and helped her good friend to rise, also begging him to leave the chamber of death, and endeavour to seek rest.

"Rest, my dear girl," he replied, mournfully. "Where shall I rest—there is no more rest on earth for me, till I—till I rest with my sainted child," and his voice trembled as he spoke. He could say no more; but there was such utter misery in those words, that the young heart of his companion was powerfully affected; and she whispered softly and soothingly as she fondled his hand in hers—

"Is there not a deep and holy joy in looking forward to that blessed time when we shall meet again, and behold her far brighter and happier than when we knew her here, and when we shall dwell together in the realms of eternal bliss, in that glorious home above, and never again be separated from her. Oh! my dear kind friend, let us look forward to that. Is there not joy and soothing in that hope. Yes—yes, it is a holy and a most joyful thought. Let us then, not forget our duties to the living while we are on earth; and then, depend on it, our reward will be found with her.

In a low, subdued tone, it was thus that Maud spoke; and her words fell not unheeded. They fell on a Christian's ear—a true Christian, to whom the Redeemer—our only Intercessor—was his hope and his strength.

The poor father suffered his young friend to lead him from the chamber of death without a murmur—she had softened the agony of his grief, and her words had comforted him.

## CHAPTER XVI.

A WEEK had passed away since the day of Edith's death, and the time had arrived when her mortal remains were to be laid in their last resting place. It was not in Bridgnorth she was to be buried, but in a cemetery about a mile and a half from that town.

Who would not rather see loved relatives laid in a country burial ground, with the green turf for a covering, where daisies spring up to deck their graves, in beautiful simplicity, where the pure winds of heaven sweep over the little mounds, and where the sweet refreshing rains descend and keep them constantly verdant, than in the thickly-clustered graves of a large town burial ground? In the former, the parents or the friends of the departed can visit the place free from interruption, and there is certainly a melancholy pleasure in going to the spot where the remains of a loved one lies, in planting flowers around it, and watching them bloom in beauty over the peaceful grave.

The cemetery was lovely situated on an eminence, and received all the winds of heaven in their mighty force as they swept across the country. The view from this spot was charming, and was one poor Edith had often visited and admired for its tranquillity, and here it was she was laid.

Her body had not been removed from Mrs. Courtenay's house, so those who attended the funeral assembled there. In the mourning-coaches were General Ryan and his son-in-law, the Rev. Mr. Raymond, Cecil Woodhouse and the doctors, Sir Harry Boothby and his brother, the latter pale as marble. Thus they proceeded to the cemetery, and when they had deposited the remains of poor Edith in their last resting place, they returned, the unhappy father to his now desolate home, and the rest to their respective abodes. Shortly after the return of Sir Harry and Augustus, a carriage drove up to Mrs. Courtenay's door to convey Mrs. Gibson and her daughter to their home.

Maud had gone to her own room, for she longed to be alone that her tears might flow unwitnessed. The sorrow she had looked upon during the past week had entered her heart, and the fountains of her soul gushed forth like gentle rivulets flowing over and refreshing the hard, dry soil through which they pass. She remained alone till evening, and then she remembered there was another who required comforting, and that it was her duty to do all she could to soothe his wounded spirit and console him. She bathed her face to remove all traces of crying, left her chamber, and slowly and wearily proceeded towards the drawing-room.

It was evening, and though the moon shone brightly in through the windows, Maud did not perceive that although her mother and Lady Boothby and Sir Harry were there,

Augustus was absent. On her entering the room Sir Harry rose hastily, went forward to meet her, and, taking her hand, whispered earnestly—

"Have you been to see poor Augustus, dear Maud?"

"No," she said, and a feeling of shame came over her for her selfishness. "Has he thought me very unkind?" and tears again rushed to her eyes?

"No, no, my dear, not unkind; only he inquired for you two or three times. Will you go to him now?"

"Where is he?"

"In the breakfast room."

"I will," Maud said, in a low, subdued tone, returning the kind pressure of Sir Harry's hand. She immediately left the room.

Yes, there was Augustus, alone in the breakfast room, stretched on a couch, his eyes closed, as if in sleep. His heart had been tortured with agony that day, and indeed every day during the past week, since that fatal truth had been disclosed to him—that truth which had been so fearful a shock. Yes, agony; for he had beheld the father's crushing sorrow for his loved child. Augustus could not hide from himself the fact that he, in great measure, had accelerated the death of that child. It is true he was aware she had always been in delicate health; but he was also aware intense sorrow had brought on that decline which had hurried her into an early grave. Unconsciously—Heaven was his witness—he had caused that sorrow; but he could not divest himself of the conviction that he had, in some measure, contributed to render the aged father's remaining days desolate and lonely. Feeling, however, is a thing that cannot be reasoned against, it were folly and idle to attempt it.

Mr. Boothby had remained in the breakfast room since his return from the funeral, and none had entered there save his brother, for the reason of his great grief had in some measure, by this time, become known to all. In fact Lady Boothby and Mrs. Courtenay had been conversing on the subject, and Julia had told her husband the sad tale, which caused the latter sad sorrow. Maud quietly entered the room, and as gently approached the couch on which he lay, pale and still as a prostrate statue. His arms were folded on his breast, and his dark hair was pushed completely off his forehead. Maud quickly glided to his side, and kneeling beside him, lightly kissed his brow. Augustus started, and at the same time opening his eyes, beheld Maud. For an instant a flash of joy illumined his expressive face, but almost as quickly vanished, leaving the stamp of dark misery impressed upon his every feature. He arose and clasped his affianced wife to his heart in one impassioned embrace, and he put her from him, and with his arms again folded on his bosom and his head turned aside, in a low voice, tremulous from emotion, said—

"Maud, can you consent to become my wife now? Can you love the man who has hastened, perhaps caused the death of an innocent fellow-creature, and robbed her aged father of the sole comfort of his declining years? Can you look upon me with other feelings than those of disgust and loathing? In a word, can you regard me as you were used to do?"

So spoke the proud man, who had never before humbled himself to a single human being. There was one by his side who was equally proud and unbending, and she well knew the cost those words had been to him to utter, aye, even to her. Maud had a generous heart, and she lost not an instant in hastening to comfort him in his overwhelming grief.

"Augustus, dearest Augustus," she cried, as she placed her hands on his, "listen to me. Your conduct was not what you represent it; you are very sensitive, and have exaggerated an unconscious error into a wilful sin. In the first place you were not the cause of poor Edith's death. Sorrow, no doubt, accelerated it; but I firmly believe, and so do others, as well as the doctor, that disease was always making its slow progress in her frame. Besides, my love, you knew not that she had given you her young heart. You had not sought it, though the poor girl imagined you had. My feelings towards you are the same as they have ever been, and I respect and esteem you now as truly as I did when I knew not of this mournful affair in which you have been so painfully involved. Yes, perhaps you are even dearer to me; for the past week has proved how intensely sensitive is your nature, how delicate are the fibres of that mind I have so loved to study and commune with; I have discovered that, with all your apparent hauteur and outward coolness, how tender is your heart, how open to the softest, tenderest, purest sensibilities. I knew it all, my dear one, long, long ago; but the past week has proved me right. Come, Augustus, do not look so sorrow-stricken. We must mourn for the dear girl. Nature will have it so; but it is a selfish grief, after all, for she is now supremely happy, rejoicing with the angels above. Nor can we help mourning for the sorrowing father. But think you not that even *his* deep sorrow will ere long be changed into joy. It is the shock, and the suddenness of that shock, and the great desolation of his home that causes his grief to be so mighty for the present; time will abate its intensity, for my dear old friend is a good man, and a true Christian, and will soon perceive how merciful God has been to his poor child, as well himself, in removing her from the trials and sufferings which, had she lived, her disease would have engendered. Yes, he will soon have to look forward with hope and joy to the time when he will meet her again, never more to part. Have I not spoken truth? Yes, it is so; then ask me not again, if I can look upon you with other feelings than those of disgust and loathing. I thought you knew me better; you do—you must; those were but passionate words, uttered at a moment of the most poignant suffering."

The expression of deep despair vanished from the poet's face, as a thunder-cloud before the sun, as Maud's words fell upon his ears; and though joy and gladness did not appear, there was a look of intense gratitude mingled with his great love, that was beautiful to behold.

Taking her hand in his, and pressing her to his heart, he said—

"My Maud—my life, how can I thank you for those words of love and tenderness. You are right in saying I spoke but in passion just now, when I said I thought you would regard me with altered feelings; for my own darling, if you had said you could not become my wife; if you had told me that all respect, all affection for me was gone, I really think I should have lost my senses; far greater would have been the misery than any I hitherto ever knew, and Heaven knows that has been heavy indeed. Oh! Maud, darling, you can form no idea of the extent of my love. You, and you only, could have humbled my pride, have checked my besetting sin; to you alone could I bend; and to be cast out from your heart, to be sent from you now, would have rendered my life unbearable, Maud, when heart meets a kindred heart, they should never be separated."

The conversation was continued for some time,

and Maud's words gave a balm to her lover's regrets. Little, however, did he imagine or suspect that at the time she was using her utmost powers to rouse him from his distress, her heart was rent by an overwhelming sorrow, which she believed could never pass away. With all the poet's study of the human heart, he had failed to discover Maud's secret grief.

## CHAPTER XVII.

In an early chapter of this history it will be recollected by our readers that Mrs. Courtenay was described as somewhat of an exacting mother, and we regret we have to recount another conversation in which she too plainly shows herself as such.

During the past week, Mrs. Courtenay had been told by Lady Boothby the cause of the agitation and sorrow of her brother-in-law on the death of Edith Ryan. Common delicacy, as well as mourning for the departed one, had prevented Mrs. Courtenay from speaking to her daughter on the subject; but the funeral over, the first shock passed away, she thought it was time to seek and have an explanation of the whole affair. She also had other matters on which she wished to converse with her daughter, and which lately she had not had an opportunity of doing.

It was the day following that of the funeral that she entered Maud's bed-room. It was somewhat late in the afternoon. Maud was busily engaged reading. To her mother's knock at the door and inquiry if she might come in, Maud replied—

"Come in, dear mamma."

Mrs. Courtenay entered the room, and took a seat beside her daughter.

"I am not wanted, am I?" the daughter asked, kissing her mother's cheek.

"No, my love; they are all in the drawing-room."

"How are they engaged?"

"Sir Harry and Julia are reading, and Augustus is engaged, writing letters."

Mrs. Courtenay's face assumed a graver and a somewhat sterner expression, as she continued—

"It is of Mr. Boothby I wish to speak to you, Maud. I have long wanted to do so; but the death of poor Edith has, of course, prevented me. Now, however, I think it is quite right I should."

"Well, dear mamma, what have you to say?" asked Maud.

"When you first named your engagement, I gave my consent, which indeed you scarcely asked for, believing that in so doing I was ensuring your happiness and future welfare. Once or twice since that time, a doubt has come across my mind; but it is not of that I wish now to speak. It is of the sad affair of poor Edith, and the—disgraceful part—I cannot help saying it—that your intended husband took in it. Maud, he killed that poor child!"

"Mamma!" interrupted Maud, "what do you mean?"

"What do I mean," repeated Mrs. Courtenay, "exactly what I say; he killed that poor child. I am confident of it, and I fear, indeed I am almost certain that he is one of those men who are met with so often in fashionable society, who break the hearts of many innocent girls, and then finally marry one who does not care for them in the least, and pretty sort of husbands such men make. I trust, my love, you will have the good sense never to try."

Maud heard her mother's words, but so astonished was she, that she almost doubted the evidence of her senses. Her mother's abruptness grated harshly on her heart; but she showed it not in her countenance, though she could not help replying haughtily—

"Am I to understand, mamma, that it is your wish I should break my engagement with Augustus?"

"On that point you must decide for yourself," replied Mrs. Courtenay; "but were I a girl I would never marry a man who had done everything in his power to win another girl's love and then desert her, especially if he had gone to such lengths as being the death of her. No, Maud, if you value your future peace of mind, break off your engagement at once. Don't talk to me about talent and poetry and such stuff, what use are they if the man possessing them has no heart, no proper regard for our sex. In this instance, I am pretty certain he would make nothing but unhappiness for you. Oh! my dear child, I wish you had never gone to that sink of iniquity, London. I always had my fears that some harm would come of your going there. I had rather a thousand times you had married your cousin, Cecil Woodhouse, than this Augustus, with all his talent and genius. Oh! how do I wish you had married Woodhouse."

"Mamma, mamma, what are you saying?" said Maud, in a scarcely audible voice, not tremulous from emotion but from passion. "How dare you utter such words against Augustus, the noble and the good. You are quite mistaken in his character. He never trifled with Edith, and he is all amiability and goodness."

"You may say what you please, Maud," cried her mother passionately, "I will never believe that he did not trifle with that darling child."

"Nevertheless, what I say is the truth," continued Maud firmly; "he never even suspected she loved him, nor did he ever seek to win her love. Some one has given you a false version of the story, and placed Augustus's character in a totally wrong as well as unfavourable a light."

"No, Julia gave me the same version that you have done," replied Mrs. Courtenay, "but I can plainly see through it all. I don't blame Lady Boothby for glossing over her brother-in-law's faults and doing all she can to conceal and soften his unmanly conduct towards poor Edith. Neither she nor any one else can deceive me. You need no other evidence than the depth and intensity of his agitation at her death to prove the truth of the matter."

"Mamma, mamma, say no more," pleaded her daughter.

"I must say all I think, Maud,; I don't mean that his heart is entirely hardened, for he showed that he was secretly aware of his baseness, and when it was too late he was sorry for what he had done."

"Cannot you understand, mamma, that a high

and sensitive nature, may, and indeed would, deplore most sincerely, the sorrow of which he had been the unconscious cause."

" Unconscious !" repeated Mrs. Courtenay.

" Yes, unconscious," continued her daughter; " do you imagine that it is only the guilty who suffer. No, mother, not they alone. Augustus could have known no misery equal to that he endured the last week."

" Not greater misery than his heartlessness deserved."

" I tell you again and again, mamma, he has not been guilty of the sin of which you accuse him."

Thus it was that Maud defended the conduct of her betrothed husband; her cheek flushed and her dark eye kindled proudly.

" Well," said the mother, " you are as wilful, Maud, as Mr. Boothby is heartless. I have done my duty by warning you; so now you must take your own course. I only trust that you will not have occasion to repent it. I must confess I did hope I should love the man you selected for a husband as if he were my own son; but I can never love Mr. Boothby. I knew from the first day I saw him I never could, although then I thought much better of him than a longer intimacy has since enabled me to do."

"What has he done to cause your dislike, mamma?"

"It is not so much what he has done as what he is," replied Mrs. Courtenay, angrily. "Sometimes his manner is cold and haughty, and then he says such bitter, satirical things; there is, too, a look of conscious superiority about him that I utterly dislike. He is so vain of his talents. For my part, if I were going to marry a man I had rather he possessed less head and more heart. I have tried hard to understand Mr. Boothby, but cannot."

A slight sneer curled Maud's lips, as she said in reply—

"Do not attempt to understand Augustus Boothby, mamma; you will never succeed. A man of Mr. Boothby's talent can never be vain. He is far above such paltriness, and ascribes all his greatness to God!"

"Oh, no doubt," sneered Mrs. Courtenay, "he is something very wonderful. Give me Cecil Woodhouse: he has none of these vanities, no self-laudations. I can understand him."

"Do you think so?" said Maud.

"I don't think I can, for I am quite certain."

"Well, then, mamma, remain happy in the belief," said Maud, a peculiar smile again curling her lip.

"I intend doing so; and as to Mr. Boothby—"

"I shall make no further attempt," interposed Maud, with a quiet but somewhat cold firmness, "to exonerate him from the charges you have brought against him, for I deem it little less than an insult to suppose it requisite. But I tell you once and for all that I have pledged myself to become his wife, believing in his goodness, his greatness, and his nobility of mind, and seeing in him qualities such as you do not even dream of, and such as I can never meet in any other man."

"I daresay not," said Mrs. Courtenay, sneeringly; "but, Maud, are your mother's wishes to be entirely put out of the question?"

"Your wishes were consulted, and you gave your consent to our union."

"Yes, but before I knew what sort of a man he was."

"I have promised to be his wife, and I will not break my engagement even to gratify my mother's wish, arising from an unjust and unfounded charge. I respect and value him more at this moment than I did the first month I knew him."

"Well, Maud, I only hope you know him as well as you think you do."

"As I am sure I do."

"And *respect and value him*," said Mrs. Courtenay, repeating her daughter's words. "What's the use of respecting a man if you do not love him?"

"I do love as well as respect him," said Maud.

" Well, then, all I can say is, that I never saw such cold feelings as you both evince. As for you, child, you look like a statue of marble instead of being bright and happy like other girls I have seen. Why, I declare sometimes you look as if you had all the cares of the world upon you. I cannot fancy you in love, and as for Mr. Bootbby, I never saw anything in him like—like—"

" Love-making!" interrupted Maud. " Is that the word, mamma? No, and what's more you never will."

" Well, call it just what pleases you," returned Mrs. Courtenay ; " but if all great geniuses and talented people are such cold dummies as those I now see, give me persons of inferior intellect— those who have weaker heads and stronger hearts."

" No doubt they would suit you better," replied Maud, quietly.

" Well, as far as I have been able to discover, your very talented lover thinks staring into your eyes for half-an-hour without speaking is love-making."

"We are neither of us fond of making a parade of our affections to the gaze of others. If you really knew Mr. Boothby's delicate and refined mind, you would understand that his love is far down in his heart—a love that only *one* can discover."

"*You* must have been very quick-sighted to have made the discovery so speedily. I only hope you have not deceived yourself into the belief that you do love him well enough to become his wife."

Maud's delicate nature could stand this conversation no longer. This seeking for confidence was intolerable, and she felt if she encouraged its continuance a thousand questions would be asked without any regard to her feelings; she determined, therefore, at once to put a stop to all further interrogation, and said, with great firmness and a degree of hauteur—

"I am sorry to find that you possess so poor an opinion of my discretion and judgment. In future, I must request that the feelings of my heart may be allowed to remain sacred—nay, they shall."

There was a determination in her daughter's manner when she uttered these words, that deterred Mrs. Courtenay from questioning her farther; but nothing annoyed her so much, although she would not have avowed it, as being baffled in obtaining her daughter's confidence, which she thought every mother had a right to demand. So she said, while an impatient frown contracted her brow—

"Oh! I do not want your confidence; only, Maud, I wish you to understand that I consider every mother has a right to her daughter's confidence."

"I differ from you," was the quietly spoken answer.

Kind and affectionate as Mrs. Courtenay usually was, yet when her daughter displeased her she felt inclined to retaliate, and often said things which in her calmer moments she regretted. After a few minutes' silence, during which she was turning over in her mind what subject she could hit upon in order to testify her displeasure, she resumed—

"You have never told me, Maud, where you intend to live after you are married. Really I cannot imagine what sort of a wife you will make. What with your high-flown notions and your husband's head always up in the clouds, a nice piece of business you will make of it. Your house I should think will be a perfect curiosity."

Maud opened her eyes wide in genuine astonishment, as she replied—

"Has no one ever told you that it is our present intention to travel after our marriage. I know Augustus is not fond of telling people of our plans, but I really thought he had told you of our arrangements."

Mrs. Courtenay's face flushed with anger. The idea, if such a plan had ever crossed her mind, of her daughter's going abroad after her marriage, was most distasteful to her. She had always pictured to herself Maud married to a gentleman of "comfortable income," who loved his native place so that he never left it or travelled to other lands, even in imagination. She also had secretly looked forward to the time when Maud would give up writing, and sink into the ordinary, homely, domesticated housewife, and for ever have banished her high-flown notions. These were Mrs. Courtenay's picturings, and ever had been, of her daughter's married life, and a secret hope for a year or two was that Cecil Woodhouse would have been the husband her daughter would have selected, and then she (Mrs. Courtenay) would have possessed a son-in-law whom she thoroughly understood.

The pause in the conversation was broken by the mother, who said—

"I was never told of your plans before, and they appear to me wild and absurd. The idea of your going abroad on a wedding tour! It is monstrous! I had hoped you would have settled quietly down and discontinued authorship, and depend on it, Maud, if Augustus goes on, writing he will make a very sorry sort of husband."

A smile of genuine amusement rested for a

moment on Maud's features, and as it vanished she replied—

"We are not going on a mere marriage tour; our object will be to lay in a better store of knowledge, to enable us the more easily to benefit our fellow creatures by pursuing our literary career, if God wills that we ever should return. As to discontinuing to write, that I shall most assuredly never do. Even if I felt I was able to do it, I see no reason why I should, or why my husband should work and I be idle. Besides, were I to cease writing, the chief happiness of my life would be gone. Yes, start not, dear mamma, for even with the love of such a man as Augustus, my life would be void and miserable, were I to forsake what I consider my high and holy office. Mamma, what strange notions you have respecting authors. You seem to have got an idea into your head that a man whose glorious office it is to enlighten his fellow men cannot at the same time fulfil the duties of a kind and affectionate husband."

"Oh! how can they be good husbands; they

seem to have no time for domestic duties, their whole thoughts being occupied in endeavouring to gain the world's fame."

Maud's countenance was lit up by something between a sneer and a smile.

" But putting that aside, and also the disadvantage of your own time being almost entirely absorbed by study and writing," continued Mrs. Courtenay, " which of itself would unfit you for the wife of any man who had not a large fortune—"

" Stop, mamma," interrupted Maud, " you appear to forget that, though my literary labours are the great pleasure of my life, they are not worthless, even in a pecuniary sense. You forget that by the books I have already published, I have realised a considerable sum of money, and—your last speech compels me to say this—that I have not only been able to relieve you of Blanche's support, but I have also had ample means of providing myself with clothes, books, and other necessaries. Therefore, even in this lower sense, my profession is a useful one, and I look forward with hope and trust to the time when we shall make both money and fame by our writings; the former will enable us to relieve the necessities of our fellow creatures, and as for the latter God will bless us."

"That's all very fine talking," replied Mrs. Courtenay, who was determined to express her disapprobation of something, and she really spoke what she thought. "But with all that you will not be fitted to make a good wife."

"Why not?"

"Because, in the first place, you are too cold, or, I should rather say, indifferent; and, in the second place, you are not sufficiently cheerful or lively. Most men like a merry laughing face in a wife. I suppose, however, Augustus is different from all other men; there is more of bitterness than love in his composition. I cannot say I like his air of conscious superiority."

"Mamma; there you are right; his is conscious superiority, it is not vanity; that is applicable only to little minds. Yes, it is that conscious superiority that has elevated him above all around him."

" But you are so dull and mournful looking," resumed Mrs. Courtenay, who determinedly pursued the system of underrating her daughter, though she literally meant what she was now saying, only if Maud had not displeased her she would not have given it utterance. " You are so different and always were to other girls; you never were merry or light-hearted."

" What you say is quite true. I never was like others," exclaimed Maud, bitterly, as an expression of deep sadness passed over her features.

" I can't for the life of me see why you should not be as merry and light-hearted as other girls," resumed Mrs. Courtenay. " You have had an easy life hitherto. It is entirely your own fault if you have not been happy; you have had no sorrow, how should you."

Oh! the hollow mocking smile that rested on poor Maud's lips as she heard those words. Still, however, she made no reply, until her mother, observing a strange expression in her manner, said—

"I am sure, to look at you, no one would ever think you were in love as you term it."

"How do people look when they are in love, as *you* term it?" asked Maud, with a smile she could not suppress. "I hear you speak so much about it, that there surely must be something very extraordinary in the appearance of people in love."

"Oh! but you look so grave and solemn—almost sorrowful; anyone would suppose you were unhappy. I think, my love, if there is anything causing you grief, you ought to tell your mother. Are you sure you are quite happy? You might give me your confidence so far, at any rate; besides, I don't like anything secret between mother and daughter. I think I have a right to know all your feelings, whether they are joyful or sorrowful."

Poor Maud, she knew that here again was the commencement of a strict cross-examination of all her thoughts, feelings, and she shrunk from complying with her mother's somewhat coarse, though natural demand. This was the second time in their conversation that her mother had attempted to draw from her entire confidence, tried to induce her to yield up every sacred feeling of her heart, and a sense of wretchedness oppressed her as she thought of this unworthiness and want of delicacy in the mother who she so tenderly and affectionately loved. She was roused, but not to anger, to reply to her mother.

"I quite agree with you, mamma, that there should be every confidence between a mother and daughter on most things; but there are times when a daughter cannot, ought not - a mother has no right always to expect or demand confidence, if by it you mean that no feeling of her heart is to be kept sacred, no thought of her mind unspoken—why should she gratify the questionings of even a mother, who would drag forth the most sacred feelings of the heart. I believe you have never found me, to use your own words, 'underhand' in my conduct, but if by the term, you infer that I do not freely lay bare my innermost thoughts and feelings for inspection and comment, I plead guilty to the charge; that I never have done, never will, or can do—I see it is time to dress for dinner."

"Well, my dear," said Mrs. Courtenay, who felt certain there was no hope of gaining her point, "I am very glad you understand your future husband, for I candidly confess I do not. I hope you know and feel that the dearest wish of my heart is for your happiness, and I also hope that as your entire trust is placed in Augustus, he will make you a good husband."

Rising from her chair, she kissed her daughter as she passed her chair, and left the room.

"Would that I were worthy of his love," were the low spoken and heart-rending words that fell from the poor girl's lips as the door closed.

## CHAPTER XVIII.

WEEKS and months had passed since the events recorded in our last chapter, and still the Boothbys remained at Belle Vue Cottage. The first heavy grief and mourning for poor Edith Ryan had passed away from the hearts of all save her aged father, and even he felt, like the rest, that his child was in a happier home, and rejoiced in that happy thought; but to him she had been the one bright star of his existence, the sole joy and comfort of his declining years. He could not rally from the sudden shock, and almost immediately after the funeral he went to the Raymond's, and had remained with Ellen and her husband ever since, they doing everything to

M 5

alleviate his deep grief that loving hearts could devise, Ellen had persuaded her father to remain with her until after Christmas.

In consequence of Edith's death, the marriage of Maud and Augustus had been postponed to the spring.

Cecil Woodhouse had been a frequent visitor at Mrs. Courtenay's, but of course much of his time had been spent at Easton with his affianced bride; for though his heart was with another, his high sense of honour would not allow him to remain in that other's society longer than was absolutely requisite to avoid observation. He had used every effort to render Dora happy and free from all uneasiness, and so well had he succeeded, that the girl implicitly believed in his love, and her heart rejoiced in it.

When Woodhouse was in Maud's presence, he could not avoid gazing into her dark mournful eyes, although he feared some word or look might betray the secret of his heart. Hitherto, both had managed to assume a manner which was foreign to their feelings, but Maud's long absence from home had had a powerful influence on her cousin, and when she returned, his love, too, returned with increased warmth. He knew how he wronged Dora when he was in the enthralling presence of Maud, and he repented his direlection of duty the moment he left her.

What strange creatures are we all, the very best of us are but erring mortals, liable to be led away from the paths of right in an evil hour. But Maud and Woodhouse were different to those who go about wilfully and deliberately sinning, who, once beginning a career of vice, steadily pursue it, listening neither to the voice of reason nor of kindness.

\*　　\*　　\*　　\*　　\*　　\*

The morning preceding Christmas-day was cold, bleak, without a ray of sunshine. Maud had dressed herself for a walk and was just emerging from the hall door, her cloak muffled closely around her, when she encountered Augustus Boothby, who was coming up the garden walk.

"Oh! Maud. I am just in time to walk with you. Where are you going?"

A slight colour tinged Maud's face, as she replied—

"I am sorry to refuse your kind offer, Augustus; but I must go alone on my present expedition!"

There was something in the girl's manner that startled her lover—a confused appearance that was totally foreign to her, and he said, with some slight impatience—

"If your errand is such that you can venture alone, why should you blush to name it; or rather, why shrink from doing so at all?"

Maud looked up into her companion's face astonished, and she replied with a slight shade of hauteur, which came involuntarily, when she felt that the least shade of suspicion or distrust was attached to her movements—

"I cannot name it to you, Augustus; I am under a promise never to mention to any one visits, of which this is one, that I am obliged to pay. Nor can I name the place to which I am going!"

"Very well; then I am to understand that there are secrets between us of a serious nature. You do a thing which you shrink from naming. Maud, I warn you to be careful."

With a quick step he turned away, and entered the house, and Maud proceeded on her mission, she was too proud to seek even him and tell him she had made that promise to secresy long before she had ever seen him. That promise was made to poor Blanche, that she would never mention to anyone staying at Bellevue her name or abode. How strange it is that there are periods, when even the most trifling circumstances will perplex the mind, whilst at any other time they would have not the least effect. It was so with Augustus to-day. It was the first word that had ever passed his lips to Maud except those of love and kindness. He scarcely knew what prompted him to speak so bitterly to her; perhaps it was a fancied strangeness in her manner. It must have been a combination of causes, for he had a mind far above those who consider it the duty of an affianced wife to divulge the secrets of a third party. He would have scorned such thoughts, but there are impulses in the human breast that can never be described in words, that we ourselves can scarcely understand, but incomprehensible as they are, they prompt conduct that, perhaps, afterwards we sadly repent. Truly, Augustus could not define his feelings, or explain to himself the cause of having used such harsh words, in his impatience, to Maud this morning.

Maud proceeded to Nelly Briggs' cottage. She walked rapidly along, and her thoughts during the walk were of the most painful nature ; as she thought over Augustus's harsh words, and conduct so unlike himself, a severe pang pierced to her heart and caused the cold feeling of loneliness and desolation of other days to return with redoubled force. She had visited Blanche many times since her return home, but had never before chanced to encounter Mr. Boothby or any other person to question her as to where she was going or the nature of her errand.

When in Blanche's presence, Maud subdued all

her wretched feelings; but as she talked to the poor penitent girl and witnessed the holy calm that pervaded her mind, her own sad spirit to a certain extent left her as she reflected, "If she is thus calm and peaceful, surely I ought to be so likewise."

"Dear Maud," said Blanche, as she rose to leave her, "may you spend many happy Christmas times; I, of all others, should wish it, for you have been my guardian. You have comforted me—you have soothed me. You have proved to me that, great a sinner as I have been, I need not despair. Oh! Maud, surely your prayers have been heard."

"Blanche, God is ever ready to hear the prayers of the sorrowful. Thank not me, for to Him alone is thanksgiving due. Let your future life testify your gratitude, and there can be no more fitting season of the year in which to be thankful than the morrow—the anniversary of the birth of our blessed Lord our only intercessor. Good-bye, Blanche, God bless you."

"God bless you, dear, good Maud," said

Blanche, the tears falling fast down her cheeks. "May your kindness to me be returned to you tenfold. Good-bye! Oh! how I have learnt to love you."

Maud descended the stairs to the kitchen of the cottage, soothed by Blanche's words, and thankful that she had been the humble instrument in inducing the wilful girl to a state of thorough repentance. To her consternation when she entered Nelly Briggs's tidy kitchen, Cecil Woodhouse was sitting by the fire chatting with the worthy woman.

"My dear Maud, who would have thought of seeing you out in such a day and such an hour as this?" were Woodhouse's words of greeting, as he rose to shake hands with her.

"It has come on to snow since I came here, and I have staid much longer than I had intended," she replied.

"Please sit down, Miss Maud," said Nelly; "and warm yourself, for I am sure you must be cold. It is very fortunate Mr. Woodhouse is here to walk home with you," continued the good woman, placing a chair close to that on which Cecil had been sitting in front of the blazing fire.

There was no ceremony with Nelly and her visitors, each appeared as if they thought only of the present hour; they seemed to be carried back to that time when both were free from engagements. This very unexpected and sudden meeting with Woodhouse had thrown Maud completely off her guard for awhile. Cecil, too, had only just been told by Nelly that his cousin was upstairs with Blanche, and before he had time for thought she entered the kitchen. Neither had time to recover themselves, and put on, as they had been compelled to do of late, the hateful mask now so familiar to them. This was the first hour in their life that the faintest glimmer of truth dawned upon their minds, and now a strange light began to break in upon each.

"I fear you are very cold, Maud," said Woodhouse, as he observed the intense paleness of her face, and the almost livid whiteness of her lips.

"Yes," she replied, "I am very cold."

Darkness was coming on, and Nelly said—

"I think, Miss, you and Mr. Woodhouse had better stay and have a cup of hot tea before you go forth into the cold. It won't take long to get ready, for the kettle is nearly boiling. You needn't mind, Miss, as Mr. Cecil is here to see you safe home."

Nelly's words fell upon the hearts of her visitors, creating an unaccountable sensation—they seemed like the music of long ago, returning once more to greet them.

Unconsciously, Cecil possessed himself of Maud's hand, which was icy cold, and pressed it between his to warm it. A thrill of strange unusual joy ran through her frame, and for a short time she forgot everything and every person but him. She made no attempt to release her hand, but in an instant the harsh words of Mr. Boothby crossed her mind, which, few as they had been, caused a sense of desolation and weariness into her young heart once more. Woodhouse's presence at that moment, and his warm pressure of her hand, seemed comfort to her troubled spirit, seemed to assure her she had a kind friend near at hand—one, too, who at times she had fancied possessed not one kind feeling towards her.

Whilst Nelly was busily engaged getting ready the tea, the visitors forgot their sorrows, and thought only of the present blissful moments. When Nelly announced that tea was ready, Maud endeavoured to withdraw her hand from Woodhouse's; but he still held it firmly clasped in his own. Then she looked up, and their eyes met. She started; there was something in the face she gazed upon that took away from her the power of turning her eyes away. She plainly saw that all affection had not vanished from his heart; but she saw not he was longing to tell her that he loved her better than life itself. Although she could not see thus much, she saw, at last, that her cousin regarded her with affection, and a sweet calm joy came over her spirit, though with that present joy was mingled a recklessness of the future.

The snow had been falling fast almost from the

moment Maud entered the cottage, and the ground was covered with its white flakes. It had now ceased, the sky had become cleared, and the moon shone out with great brilliancy, illumining the white clad landscape. The air was cold, though the wind had subsided into stillness. It was about eight o'clock when Woodhouse took leave of Nelly to set out on the homeward walk to Bellevue Cottage.

"Good-bye, Nelly," said Woodhouse and Maud at the same moment.

"Good-bye, Miss Maud, and Master Cecil; a happy and merry Christmas to you both," and each giving the kind-hearted old woman a hearty shake of the hand they left the cottage. But ere they had got three yards from the door, Nelly called out—

"Please take care of Miss Maud, Mr. Cecil, that she don't slip up on the snow. Good-bye, Miss, good-bye, sir; much obliged to you for your visit," and Nelly re-entered her snug kitchen, Maud and Woodhouse proceeding on their way.

"I will take care of her and protect her," thought Woodhouse, Nelly's words still ringing in his ears. Then he said, aloud, " Lean on my arm, dear Maud, the ground is very slippery."

The moon was shining brightly, giving a dazzling brilliancy to the snow, which covered every leafless bough, every field, every hedgerow.

" Do you remember our last walk through this lane, Maud?" asked her companion.

" Yes, perfectly," she replied; " I think the scene far more beautiful now."

" I think so, too," said Woodhouse, pressing her arm more tightly.

" Moonlight shining on a snow-clad landscape is truly lovely. Hark! there are the bells of Bridgnorth, telling that it is Christmas Eve, and bidding us rejoice."

As she spoke, the chimes of the distant bells came softly and pleasantly across the country. Everything around combined to make Maud and her cousin forget all and everything but the present hour. They had not gone far, when they heard the sound of voices issuing from a neat little cottage they were approaching. On coming nearer, a sweet voice was singing a hymn of Glory.

"Stop!" said Woodhouse, "let us listen to that simple hymn of praise and thanksgiving."

"How exquisite!" whispered Maud. "Can you not fancy it mingling with an angel's song above? Perhaps poor Edith is singing to us now. Would that I could join her!"

Woodhouse started, struck by the tone of misery as well as the strange words.

"What do you mean, Maud?" Woodhouse said. "You, who have such a prospect of happiness before you—you, whose brightest dreams are about to be realised!"

The spell was broken. Maud scarce knew what she said, or what she did; all the sorrow of her heart rushed back in an instant upon her memory. Woodhouse looked into her unmasked face, and saw misery and recklessness of the future depicted there. A sudden thought flashed across his mind—that Maud loved not the man to whom she was engaged; and his suspicions were almost confirmed by the sorrow now so strongly depicted in her face—for surely such grief could not exist if she loved the man to whom she was so shortly to be united for ever.

"Maud," he said, feeling strangely uneasy and embarrassed, "had we not better quicken our steps? We have some distance to walk, and I fear your mother will be getting uneasy about you; besides, there is another to whom you must not cause uneasiness."

A low, bitter laugh escaped her lips, as she replied, with a strange recklessness in her tone—

"Oh! never mind; surely for once I may be free. Besides that *one*, if you mean Augustus Boothby, will not trouble himself about me."

"Not if you were under his own protection."

"Am I not under protection as secure as his could be?"

"Yes, dear Maud, quite, if not more secure," said her companion, a thrill of unspeakable pleasure thrilling through his heart.

No further mention was made of Mr. Boothby. They went on conversing on other themes, both forgetting the ties that separated them from each other, for recklesness possessed Maud that night, and she thought only of him upon whose arm she was leaning and whose hand clasped hers.

The clock from one of the Bridgnorth churches struck nine just as they arrived at Bellevue Cottage.

"Here we are, at home," said Woodhouse.

"Many thanks, Cecil, for your great kindness in conducting me here."

"Blessings on you, dear Maud," he whispered, and his voice, low as it was, his companion perceived was tremulous.

"Come in, Cecil, come in and see mamma," said Maud, as she reached the door.

Woodhouse prevented her knocking, as he held her hand firmly in his own.

"Maud," he said passionately, "will you always speak as kindly to me as you have done this night. Will you be once more to me as you used to be long ago?"

"Long ago," repeated Maud to herself, and a thousand pleasing memories floated in her brain, and all else but her companion was forgotten; "I would be, Cecil," she said aloud, in the most affectionate and tender voice.

Woodhouse raised her hand to his lips, and kissed it passionately and then released it. She knocked at the door and in a minute it was opened by the servant.

"Goodness gracious, Miss Maud, how glad I am to see you safe back again; my poor mistress has been in such a dreadful way about you, and Sir Harry and his lady have both been frightened at your absence, and as for poor Mr. Boothby, he has looked pale as death ever since you left home, but not a word has he spoken. If we'd have known Mr. Woodhouse had been with you we'd have known he would have taken every care of you."

The girl stepped aside to let them pass, and before they had crossed the hall Mrs. Courtenay came down stairs, exclaiming,

"My dear child, where have you been! I am so glad to see you back again. Where have you been? Oh! Cecil, if I had known she had been with you, I should have been sure she was quite safe."

"I have been to Nelly's cottage," said Maud, "and was detained much longer than I expected. Fortunately whilst I was there Cecil came in, and he very kindly brought me home."

"Thank you, Woodhouse, it was very kind of you to walk so far in such a wretched night. Come to the drawing-room."

Mrs. Courtenay whispered to her daughter—

"Augustus is very disconcerted, alarmed I suppose. He looks deadly pale, but he has scarcely spoken to any one since you left."

Maud knew why, and hastened to the drawing-room shaking hands with Sir Harry and Lady Boothby as she passed. They were standing on the landing waiting to see who it was that was taking off his cloak and had been Maud's conductor.

Maud entered the drawing-room alone, and

found Augustus standing by the fire-place, his arms folded and his head erect. She walked quietly forward, but he advanced not a step to meet her. He remained pale and immoveable as a marble statue, and Maud felt that she had wronged him.

"Augustus," she cried, "do not look so cold and stern. Will you not speak to me?"

He heeded not her words, and she attempted to unfold his arms, but in vain. Again she spoke—

"Augustus, have I done wrong? Must I indeed break my promise to another to explain to you the cause of my long absence to-day."

"Certainly not," he said haughtily, "though you have, it appears, communicated the nature of your errand to another man and secured his protection home."

Maud knew her conduct must have appeared very strange, and the still small voice of conscience told her she had wronged him. She was about to speak again, when Sir Harry entered the room and was being followed by the rest. Hastily she ran to Sir Harry and said in a low voice—

"Give me a few minutes with Augustus alone. I must speak to him."

"Do, Maud," replied the baronet, in an equally low whisper; "I will take Julia and the others to the dining-room for a time. Be careful, bear with him and remember his great trial in early life. It is the recollection of that which causes his very soul to sicken now," and before the rest could reach the door it was closed and Maud was alone with Augustus, who had not moved hand or foot since she first entered the room.

"Augustus," she said, again approaching him, "you must not, you shall not think that my cousin knew I was going to that place to-day. Will you listen to me?"

"Certainly, if you wish me," were the cold and haughty words she received in answer. They stung her to the very soul, but she conquered her feelings and proceeded—

"Well, then, there is—" pride induced her to hesitate and a slight colour tinged her face; in an instant, however, she continued, "yes, I must tell you all. There is a cousin of mine who used to reside with us. She was young and frivolous, her character was weak, though far from radically bad, and her intellect was of a very common order. A young officer, a friend of my brother's, was constantly here who attracted her admiration. He was her ruin—she—she fell." The girl's proud head was bent, and lower and lower it sunk as she spoke these words. " After a few weeks spent with him—I know not where—she returned nearly broken-hearted ; she remained here only a day or two, till we could place her at the cottage of a respectable and highly esteemed servant of my Cousin Woodhouse, or rather one who had lived with his father. There the poor girl has lived ever since. Perhaps some of the happiest hours of my life are those in which I reflect that I may have been in some slight degree instrumental in leading her to repentance. To-night she was more than usually affected, and I could not leave her till I saw her calm again. Besides, at this season of rejoicing—rejoicing in the true and holy sense I mean—I could not bear to think of her, penitent as she is, alone without a friend to cheer her, so I spent as much of Christmas Eve with her as I could; indeed I noticed not the flight of time, or the fast approaching darkness, till I rose to take leave. Having done so, I found my cousin Woodhouse below talking to his old servant, who he so highly respects. Had he not been there I should not have hesitated walking home alone as the moon was shining so brightly, but as he chanced to come I accepted his protection. Now, Augustus, tell me, have I fully explained myself? There should be no misunderstanding between us."

"Nor is there, dear Maud," replied the proud man, unbending at last, "I respect you more than ever I did. I love you more dearly for your charity—a quality so seldom found in women—to a fallen and degraded sister. Oh! my love, condemn me not for my harshness to you this day; for though I doubted you not—as soon would I have doubted the existence of my own soul—yet I was mystified, and the memory of other days recurred to me, and though I should no more think of placing you on a level with that woman, who for years drove every feeling of gentleness from my heart, than I should class the pure heavens with the foul earth; yet I trembled lest my only treasure should be lost to me. Maud, my love for you is almost too great for happiness, fear is too often mingled with it."

Maud felt it was so, and it deeply pained her that she could not give back the same deep love to him; she knew her life had been a *woman's error*, and in very sorrow she laid her head upon his bosom and wept. Augustus, however, little imagined whence came those tears; he gazed upon her face and saw nothing but love and gentleness beam from her eyes.

## CHAPTER XIX.

Christmas had come and gone, and poor old General Ryan had settled again in his desolate home. Two days after his return Maud said to Augustus—

"Mamma has been to call on General Ryan; shall we go and see him to-day?"

"Most willingly," replied Augustus, "but—but will he not look upon me with bitterness? Will not my presence recall painfully to him the circumstances connected with poor Edith's death?"

Maud did not reply for a moment or two; then said—

"I think not. But if you fear that I will go alone."

"At any rate I will walk to the house with you,

I can remain in the room below while you go up to the drawing-room to see him."

The day was fast fading when they started, for as the distance was short Maud did not heed its being nearly dusk. As arranged, Augustus remained in the dining-room, whilst Maud ascended to the drawing-room. The General was sitting by the firelight, which threw a warm, rich glow over the room. He was reclining in an easy chair, in an almost dreamy state, one hand supporting his white head, the other thrown listlessly over the arm of the chair.

Maud softly approached him, and putting her arms round his neck, kissed his forehead.

"Ah! is that you, my dear Maud?" cried the old man, drawing her fondly towards him. "How are you, my love?"

"Quite well, thank you, my dear, kind friend."

"It is very good of you, my love, to come and see me in my solitude and desolation."

"The very time when my presence is most needed."

"Yes, very true—very true, my dear child," said the old man, tears springing to his eyes as he thought of the dear one he had lost, and his head rested on the young girl's shoulder.

Maud spoke not; she knew his grief would sooner calm by silence than by any words she might speak, however loving they might be. She was right, for in a few minutes he rallied and said—

"I had forgotten, my love, to ask how—how Mr. Augustus Boothby is."

"Quite well, thank you," replied Maud, gravely.

"Did you walk here alone?"

"No, Augustus came with me."

"Came with you, my love! Where is he?"

"In the dining-room."

"Why does he not come to see me?" asked the General.

"He thought—he feared—"

"I know what you would say, my dear," cried her companion. "I supposed you, at any rate, would have known me better. Send for him; I would have him see that I attach no blame to him."

Maud rose to ring the bell, but the General took her hand, saying—

"Wait a short time, my love. Let me get quite calm. Sing one of your soothing songs first. I love to hear you sing. Your voice reminds me of her, only it is a little sadder, except —except just before she died."

Over the piano was a portrait of Edith, which had been painted only a few weeks before her death. Maud gazed intently up at it with deep emotion, and turning her head, saw the aged and grief-stricken father looking up at it with tearful eyes. Guessing the nature of his thoughts, she played a soft, short prelude, and then commenced singing one of the plaintive songs Edith was so fond of.

The last low notes had scarcely died away on Maud's lip, when she heard near her, but not in the direction of her aged listener, a deep drawn sigh, and looking up saw, leaning against the open door, Augustus Boothby, who had come up stairs attracted by the music.

Maud rose, and going to him, took his arm, and led him towards the General. The aged man was too much affected to speak, but he extended his hands to Augustus, who, pressing them warmly and gratefully, said in a low voice—

"Thank you, my friend, for your generous kindness. May God bless you for it."

The General soon recovered his composure.

" I hope, my dear Maud, you will soon come again. That song was very beautiful. I had almost said heavenly, it had a most extraordinary effect upon my spirits. It calmed me."

Maud rose, and kissed her kind old friend's cheek, whilst a sense of unalloyed happiness thrilled through her heart ; she was grateful to God for having given her the power of ministering consolation and comfort to a fellow-creature.

Augustus and the General conversed together for some time, and when they parted a promise was given to come again very soon. These visits were repeated almost daily, and Augustus talked with, and Maud sang and played to, the poor old gentleman, and all were comforted by these meetings.

## CHAPTER XX.

THE snows of winter have vanished, the spring has come in with bright and sunny days, and Mrs. Courtenay, her daughter and Lady Boothby were sitting at breakfast, when the postman entered the garden gate, bringing with him two letters, one for Lady Boothby and the other for Maud.

"Augustus and Sir Harry are coming tomorrow," said Maud, looking up from her letter.

"So my husband tells me," said Lady Boothby. And the two ladies kept silence reading the rest of their letters.

Whilst Maud and her friend were perusing their letters, a note was brought in and given to Mrs. Courtenay, which was immediately opened.

"This is very delightful," said Mrs. Courtenay.

"What is very delightful?" asked Lady Boothby.

"This note is from Cecil Woodhouse, asking us to go this morning and spend a long day at Pentlow Hall, entreating us to start as soon as we can, and he will walk to meet us."

"We shall of course stay all night, and come back in the morning to breakfast," said Maud.

"That will be delightful," added her ladyship, and they immediately went to their respective rooms to dress for the walk.

Before Maud had completed her toilet, her mother entered the room.

"Maud, my love, what did Augustus say in his letter?"

"Very little. He says town is beginning to fill, and that he and his brother will come by an early train, so as to be with us at dinner."

"May I not read his letter?" asked the mother.

"I think not, mamma," the daughter replied, with a smile, "Augustus only intended it for me."

"Why, if what you tell me is all he says, I should say he does not show too much affection for you."

"He is never very sentimental or demonstrative in his letters, for which I am very thankful."

"Well, I think you might show me this letter. Indeed, as your mother, I think you ought to do so."

"Excuse me, but I differ from you. I have told you all that is of consequence," Maud replied, in a haughty tone.

"I suppose he does not condescend to mention me?"

"Oh! yes; he sends his kindest regards to you. But, mamma, I do not think you are justified in asking to see his letters; nor should I be justified in showing them to you."

"Oh! just as you please—just as you please," was the testy reply. "Pray make haste down; Julia is waiting for us." And she quitted the room.

About twelve o'clock the ladies started for their walk, and Mrs. Courtenay and Lady Boothby were soon engaged in conversation, whilst Maud lingered on her way to pluck the lovely hedgerow wild flowers. The party had not gone far ere they met Woodhouse, who seemed delighted to see them. Maud somewhat dreaded the idea of going to Pentlow Hall; she retained a vivid recollection of the scene between herself and Augustus on Christmas Eve. Nor could she obliterate from her mind Woodhouse's strange manner on several occasions since that memorable walk home with him from Nelly Briggs' cottage. But as they walked on chatting and laughing, his rich, manly voice ringing in her ear, she forgot all about the past, revelling only in the present.

It had been arranged that they should have an early dinner, so that they might stroll through the garden and grounds. The hours passed pleasantly; after dinner when they had taken their wine and dessert, Woodhouse proposed starting for their ramble.

"Where are Maud and Woodhouse?" asked

Mrs. Courtenay of her companion, about twenty minutes after they had commenced their walk.

"I suppose," replied Lady Boothby, "they are gone to some particular spot. I think 1 heard Maud ask something about the shrubbery."

"Shall we seek them there?" asked Mrs. Courtenay.

"No; we may as well leave them to themselves, for no doubt they have a thousand things to talk about now they are about to be separated for so long a time. Besides," she continued, with a smile, "there is no impropriety in their being alone together; they are not acquaintances of a day, and I am sure neither Augustus nor Dora would be jealous."

The mother heaved a deep sigh, and they walked on.

Woodhouse and his cousin had unconsciously glided into earnest conversation, and lost sight of their companions, who were a little in advance of them.

"Let us turn this way," said Woodhouse; "it

leads to what used to be your favourite walk, dear Maud."

"And is still," she replied, "for independent of its quiet seclusion, there is a pleasure in looking upon spots where in days gone by we enjoyed such happy hours. When we stand on those well remembered places, we seem almost to live those few short, joyous periods over again."

Woodhouse gazed into his companion's face with astonishment, and a second time the thought crossed his mind that Maud did not really and truly love the man to whom she was about to be united. He determined to ascertain the truth of his suspicions, and said in answer to her last words—

"My dear Maud, why do you speak so mournfully, when your heart should be full of rejoicing, when Augustus—"

A somewhat bitter but low laugh escaped Maud's lips; then, as if reckless what she said, she cried in a deep passionate voice—

"Oh, God! I love him not—I esteem him as much as it is possible for one human being to esteem another; but I do not love him. Oh! Heaven, I was mad—mad when I promised to become his wife," and her eyes sparkled with an unearthly lustre as she uttered the words.

Maud had broken the ice, and Woodhouse thought not of the future or the ties that bound him to another. He remembered only those other days when he stood on that self-same spot, with his young cousin beside him, that happy time when restraint or misunderstanding had not risen between them.

"Maud," he said, in a low tone, the colour rising to his cheek and forehead, " do you remember when we last stood here together, and your young head rested on my shoulder as you spoke the strange, deep thoughts of your mind, when you would let me look down into your dear eyes."

" Cecil, Cecil, say no more."

" Maud, you must—you shall hear me. I then madly, passionately loved you, though I showed it not, and I would have given worlds to have possessed your love in return. When you came over with your mother to spend a week here, I almost believed you loved me; but, Maud, something occurred and you were cold to me and proud, and then I fancied you did not love me. Oh! my cousin, you cannot think that mighty love within my breast has died. No, no," he added, very sorrowfully, " it has burnt deeper and deeper day by day, and I have never loved another. You and you alone have had my heart's dearest regard. Maud, think of me as you will. I care not—I have unburthened my soul to you, but I never would have done so had I not heard from your own lips that we were suffering alike."

Every particle of colour left Maud's cheek as she raised her eyes to his and met his passionate gaze. All reserve was broken down between them; the passionate impulses of their hearts burst forth, recklessness of the future and almost forgetfulness of the past had taken possession of of them; yes even pride had left them. But alas! in this evil hour they had forgotten the path of duty.

Slowly Maud raised her head, and in that passionate gaze Woodhouse read the innermost depth of her heart. For a moment his emotion was too great for words, but at length he whispered, whilst his countenance was flushed from extra agitation :

"Dearest Maud, can this be true? Have you always loved me?"

"Yes, dearest Cecil, I have always loved you—love you now," and as her head sank upon his breast, she wept as she had not done for many a day.

A mighty spell seemed cast over them; Woodhouse clasped his cousin's trembling form in his arms, but for some time neither uttered a word. He kissed her forehead again and again, and everything was forgotten but the intense thrilling joy of those few fleeting minutes.

Maud was the first to break the spell. Slowly, and with a countenance compressed by mental agony, she raised her head and endeavoured to release herself from Woodhouse's encircling arms, but in vain; he clasped her the more firmly.

"Dear Cecil," she said, looking the very

picture of despair, "do you forget—it is too late—too late!"

These words, which have so often been the source of a heart's life misery startled him, he almost involuntarily released his cousin from his embrace, and drawing back a step or two said in a husky voice:

"Oh! Maud, it is indeed too late. Why did you hide from me that love which I would have given worlds to possess?"

"Cecil, do you ask me why I hid from you my love. It was pride—pride, the besetting sin of my nature; so proud was I that I scarce owned the truth to myself for—for—I believed my affection for you was uncared for—was unrequited."

"Ah! there it was," cried Woodhouse, bitterly. "We were both to blame; it was that same feeling of pride that caused me to assume an indifference so foreign to my heart. But, Maud, was it that alone which caused an estrangement to rise up between us?"

Earnestly and scrutinisingly he watched her flushed cheek.

"No, Cecil, it was not. You unconsciously, I know now, offered an insult to my intellect, which roused every particle of pride in my bosom; others also insulted me at the same time, but I cared not for them: all I cared for was your sympathy—your love. Time wore on, and the mask I had assumed to hide my grief I became accustomed to; at length I was told you loved another, that you never even mentioned my name, except with indifference, and that you never read either of my books, or took the slightest interest in me. Loving you as I did, this maddened me, and a terrible sense of utter loneliness and desolation weighed upon me, and for a time deprived me of reason. Yes, Cecil, when Augustus (who understood me as none had ever done before), when he poured forth the deep love of his poet's heart, and asked me to be his wife, I promised; but, Cecil, think not I deceived him. He knew I did not love him then; he knew that I entertained for him a sincere regard. Yes, Cecil, it was in the hour of wretchedness and desolation that I accepted him for my husband. That very night I was seized with an illness that affected my brain, and I was weeks ere I was able to leave my bed. When I recovered, a strange forgetfulness had taken possession of my mind; I seemed as if in a beautiful dream, for all remembrance of sorrow and my ill-starred attachment had for the time vanished. For weeks I continued in that blissful delusion, till as my bodily strength returned, so also did my reason, and the true state of my position burst upon me. Then I became aware that my dream was induced by a disordered brain; but not until I came back to Bridgnorth and again saw you did I know the full extent of my love for you. Yes, in madness was my faith plighted —but now my duty is to Augustus. He knew not that my reason had left me for awhile. God grant he never may."

All the time Maud had been speaking Woodhouse stood before her, his arms folded across his breast, his face pale as death, and in his eye there was an expression of misery deeper—far deeper than words can describe, than imagination can picture. He told her all that had happened during her absence, and the circumstances under which he had become engaged to Dora, and then when he had finished he took Maud's hand in his, and said, in a voice scarcely audible, so deep, so mighty was his agitation—

"Maud, we have suffered intensely—and —and—and must still; but we owe it directly to ourselves. I take the greatest blame on myself for permitting, and I may say encouraging an estrangement to rise up between us. But, my love, though we have forgotten our duty to others for an hour—I could not resist the impulse to pour out the long pent up feelings of my heart— I will not again recall this scene to you. Our lives for the future must be filled with trial and sorrow; but in the midst of grief we may glean some little joy from pursuing the path of duty. Come, Maud, let us join your mother and Lady Boothby."

## CHAPTER XXI.

THE following morning, immediately after breakfast, the ladies prepared to leave Pentlow Hall. Woodhouse, asking to be excused accompanying them, alleging, as an excuse, having to go to Easton.

Maud turned more than once as she walked through the grounds on their homeward path, to admire some of her favourite spots in the charming scenery around; and in so doing, felt sad, as she knew it was for the last time for years, if not for ever, that she, was leaving the Hall.

Sir Harry and Augustus arrived in time for a late dinner. Maud met them with a kind and cordial welcome, her thoughts reverting to that hour at Pentlow Hall with Woodhouse; she bitterly repented her departure from duty, as she met her lover's affectionate and tender gaze, and made a solemn, though silent vow, to devote every effort through life to promote his happiness, and to hide from him the sorrow of her heart. They had many things to talk about, and remained in earnest conversation the greater part of the evening. Towards the end, they spoke of their mutual acquaintances in town.

"Do you remember Miss Winstanley?" asked Augustus.

"Perfectly," Maud replied; "I admired her exceedingly. She is a highly-educated, clever girl."

"She is. Who do you think she has married?"

"Married! I never heard she was engaged."

"Yes, she was married last week to Mr. Grant, the optician."

"I am delighted to hear it, he is, in every way, worthy of her. He is no common-place man, but possesses a mind—is a man of more refinement than half those who look down upon one who, in derision, they term a shopkeeper."

"All the members of the lady's family are disgusted with the match, declaring she has not only lowered herself, but disgraced their blood."

"I honour her all the more for her discernment and spirit," said Maud, with much warmth.

"So do I. I have known and respected Grant for years, and a more upright, independent man I do not know. He will never cringe to anyone, be their rank or wealth ever so great."

"How glad I am that one, out of those victims of society, slaves to fashion, and the world's opinion, who I met during the season in town, has risen above the vulgar prejudices of her class, broken through the narrow-minded limits of aristocratic life, and dared to marry a Plebeian as they call him."

"Plebeian!" cried Augustus.

"Yes, Plebeian, not in intellect—not in mind —not in education or refinement—Plebeian, but only in the paltry matter of birth. Miss Winstanley's ancestors earned wealth by professions; Mr. Grant's in trade. This is the mighty distinction which cannot be tolerated without losing the good opinion and notice of the upper circles of civilized society. It is high time this vulgar notion of social distinction should be uprooted from among us."

"What's that you are saying?" said Sir Harry, who had heard Maud's last speech; "you are treading upon the same dangerous ground you did once before in Hyde Park. You want to do away with social distinction?"

"Yes."

"Well then, let us suppose," said Sir Harry, a good deal of fun lurking in his countenance, "you were to be married to a butcher! only think of the slaughter-house and the sheeps' heads!"

Maud and Augustus laughed heartily, and the former retorted—

"You are going beyond the mark there. A butcher could not have the qualifications I enumerated; the society in which he mixed would cause his manners to be unpolished; and this, and his occupation, would occasion a want of refinement in his tastes."

" But, my dear, explain, why I am supposing impossibilities!" persisted Sir Harry.

"If I can," replied Maud, laughing; "if I can possibly place a Grant, or a Milton, or—"

" Or an Augustus," chimed in Sir Harry, gently.

" Yes," said Maud, laughing, a faint blush tinging her cheek, " if either of these were the owners of a slaughter-house without the slightest shade of one of their glorious qualities having diminished, then I should forget the fact of the slaughter-house altogether."

Sir Harry smiled, but said no more.

" I have been thinking, Harry," said Augustus, " of the many different standards of excellence which exist amongst mankind. Few possess the same."

" And it is wisely ordained," said Maud.

" The wide difference, for instance, in Maud's standard and my own," laughed Sir Harry.

" You remember my telling you, Maud," continued Augustus, " of a man who went to the performance of a splendid opera, and sat all the evening listening most intently, not to the delicious music, but endeavouring to discover a faulty note. There was no longing in his soul for beauty; and as to intellect, it was his opinion that a man or woman was better without it, was more agreeable. This amiable gentleman—for aimable he was—was a mathematician, and condemned classics as next to useless. He was fond of the society of ladies."

" Did he marry?" asked Maud.

" I am not sure ; but I have heard him say, if he ever entered that state his wife must be good-tempered, very simple-minded, fond of household employments, and possessing a profound contempt for study of any sort; not too fond of music, but must be always merry and lively, and look up to him in all things."

" What a model for a wife!" said Sir Harry.

" I am afraid, Sir Harry, few could rise to your friend's standard of excellence," said Maud, laughing.

" Excellence !" repeated Sir Harry.

" Yes," replied Maud, musingly, " it is a strange term; but it appears to me to comprehend patience, meekness, and amiability only. There are those possessing sublimer gifts than these; but to whom patience, meekness, and amiability are denied."

" You mean to imply," said Sir Harry, "that the most highly-gifted are not always most amiable. In some cases do you not think that this, in a degree, may be accounted for?"

" Certainly I do," replied Maud, " their senses are more delicate, and their minds more sensitive."

" Has education nothing to do with these matters?" asked Sir Harry.

" Much ; I think the present system of education, more especially female education, and the usages and customs of society combine to deprave the tastes, and occasion a greater degree of frivolity in minds that cannot rise above mediocrity. Do you not think so?"

"Yes. I think education, as it is in the present day, is too frivolous, too superficial; and as to the exaggerated and absurdly affected usages of society, they go far to stifle the best impulses and most truthful and generous sentiments of the human heart."

At this moment Lady Boothby, who had been talking with Mrs. Courtenay at the other end of the room, called to her brother-in-law to come and speak to her.

"Maud," said Sir Harry. "I am glad my brother has left us for a few minutes, for I may not have another opportunity of telling you how much I enjoy your society, and how I shall miss our pleasant social chats when you leave us. It will be hard to lose my sister directly I possess her, though in the light of that dear relation I have long looked upon you."

Maud turned affectionately towards the baronet, and said with a smile—

"You have been and are, very, very kind to me, and I hope it is needless to assure you that

I have long looked upon you as a dear and highly valued friend. Your invariable kindness and affection, believe me, dear Sir Harry, is exceedingly precious."

"That is kind of you, dear Maud," said her companion with considerable emotion, for he had, in truth, become deeply attached to her, " and God grant that you and my brother may return safely from your travels, and be united to us again as one family."

Maud's face beamed with gratified feelings.

"Why, dear Maud," continued the baronet, smiling, " will you persist in putting 'sir' to my name?"

"Because," replied his companion, affectionately, " I thought you might possibly deem me disrespectful in not doing so. I shall much prefer dispensing with it if I may. Have I your permission?"

"You had it long ago, *ma chère*, so henceforth I am Harry to you if you please."

There was a pause for a minute, which was broken by Sir Harry asking—

"Maud, are we not to have some music tonight?"

"Yes, I am quite in the humour for it," affecting a gaiety which, in truth, she did not feel. "I will play as much as you like presently; but I must first persuade Julia to sing that great favourite of mine from 'Fidelio,' I will go and ask her."

## CHAPTER XXII.

WE will ask our reader to take a peep with us upon the inmates of Belle Vue cottage, the evening previous to Maud's wedding-day.

Mr. and Mrs. Raymond had arrived that morning, accompanied by Dora Gibson and her mother, the former taking up their residence at General Ryan's, the latter at Mrs. Courtenay's. It was the hour between dinner and tea, Maud and Dora had gone to the former's bedroom. Juliana, who had been engaged to accompany the bride elect abroad, and who had previously acted as lady's-maid and made herself " generally useful," was busily engaged packing her young mistress's wardrobe, which operation was nearly completed. Pausing a moment, she looked up and said—

"You have not told me, miss, what you intend putting on for travelling, after taking off your wedding dress."

"Oh! anything you like," Maud replied, "anything warm."

"Then I will leave this dress out," said Juliana, holding one up.

"That will do very well," said her mistress, impatiently.

"What bonnet do you intend wearing?" asked the maid.

"Just please yourself, I have no choice. I don't wish to be teased by such frivolous questions, as though the putting on a dress and a bonnet were matters of great importance. Carry all the things into the dressing-room and there finish your packing without asking me any further questions."

Juliana obeyed, mentally observing, with a quiet smile as she did so—

"Well, there's no accounting for what people do when they are over head and ears in love, as my young mistress is. She can think of nothing else but her future husband; it's quite natural, I suppose. I can't help thinking, though, if I were going to be married, that I should not be so careless about my dress and my bonnet, especially the bonnet. I should select one that would set off my face and head to the best advantage."

And Juliana recommenced her packing with a sigh.

"See," said Maud, turning to Dora, "what the great business of life is with some of our fellow creatures—dress! dress! Ah! that is a great mistake we women make."

"But would men be satisfied if women paid not proper attention to their dress?"

"Proper attention," Maud repeated. "Tell me, Dora, dear, do you think women dress extravagantly to please the men?"

"Not entirely."

"Not entirely! Not at all. They dress for the purpose of vieing with—of outdoing each other. It is neither more nor less than a jealous feeling and vanity in most instances."

"In most instances," replied Dora; "I am

bound to confess you are right. Too many women make dress their sole business in life. You are to be married to-morrow. Is not your business in life love?"

"Mine!" cried Maud, with a bitter smile. "Oh! Dora!" and a bright flush mounted to her forehead.

Dora looked in her companion's face with astonishment, and something akin to pain.

Maud, instantly perceiving this, said—

"I mean, my dear Dora, that the mind of a woman or a man must be weak and commonplace indeed, which could or would—to use your expression—make love the business of life. There are those, no doubt, who would call the sentiment 'hard;' but I would much rather see a man or woman devote his or her every thought and whole life to glorious efforts for the benefit of their country and the whole human race, without suffering the tender passion to enter their hearts and dwell there to the exclusion of aught else, than I would see them pass through life with love occupying their every thought."

"But, Maud dear, is not love implanted in every heart?"

"Yes, but I am speaking of that maudling feeling called love. I speak not of love of country, of kindred, of friends, of beauty, but of that morbid feeling which is so often mistaken for love, a feeling that very often, in weak-minded people, gains entire and powerful influence, and causes them to neglect the duties of life, and fix their every thought wholly on one centre. This is not right, and those are equally wrong who make love the business of life."

"But, Maud," asked Dora, "is there no allowance to be made between true love and what you term morbid love?"

"Yes, but how few know the true from the false. In many minds the spurious is as fascinating as the real, and it forms the staple of their thoughts—the business of their lives. Aye, and I fear there are those capable of loving, in the highest sense of the word, who too often unconsciously to themselves, make it the great business of their life. It is a mistake, a great error. I am thankful, dear girl, that your mind is of a higher and a stronger order."

"Are you not too sweeping in your views of young men and young ladies," said Dora, with a smile.

"Young ladies!" cried Maud. "The very term seems to me to mean dress and frivolity, vanity, and narrow mindedness, and that is, no doubt the reason why Mr. M'Gregor Allan used the epithet 'Young Ladyism.'"

"I was only in jest when I asked you, dear Maud, if love was not to be the business of your life."

"I know it was only a jest, for you, dear Dora, are a true woman and a gentlewoman in the right sense of the word, and would not make love the sole business of existence."

"I quite anticipated your answer to my question; but when you began to speak I feared I had pained you. You are right, truly happy as I am in Cecil's love, I would not allow it to monopolise my every thought. Still, Maud, I could give up all and everything for him if he wished it. Could you not do as much for Augustus?"

" I fear, my love, I am not as unselfish and amiable as you are."

" But, Maud, what is it he could ask that you would not do?"

" What I would not do he would never ask; had I married a man of a different character, greatly as I might have loved him, I would not have given up my literary pursuits, however he might have wished it. I should have felt that I was neglecting my duty to my God and my fellow creatures, if I deserted the track marked out for me, and that feeling would cause a regret in my heart, which not even love could satisfy."

" You forget, Maud, that all women are not endowed with your powerful intellect, an intellect which, if not exercised, would cause you lasting misery on earth, so that what would be selfishness in me would be far different in you. I love reading and thinking far more than all the gaieties the world can offer; but I am not so devoted to study that I could not give it up if the man I loved desired it. The case is different with you; there is planted in your breast an innate desire for knowledge, and you must seek it, as the stepping stone to happiness, and when you have attained knowledge, you feel it would be wrong not to give the benefit of your study to the world. Your feelings would give vent to something like this. It is not right; God did not intend it to be thus."

"Well done, Dora," cried Maud, looking fondly on her young companion; "you are no shallow thinker."

"Listen!" said Dora, the colour rising in her face at Maud's words, "Lady Boothby is singing one of Moore's plaintive melodies."

Both became silent, and listened in ecstasy to the melodious strains that fell upon their ears, soft as the evening breeze. Lady Boothby possessed a splendid voice, and sang with great pathos.

Maud's feelings were roused; it were impossible for any human being to be more affected by the influence of music than she was. There was only one who understood the mightly influence music had over her. Others knew that she was "fond of music," none but he could comprehend the depth of that fondness, or the greatness of that charm.

It was rarely that Maud wept, but as she sat that evening before her marriage, Dora's head resting on her shoulder, and her small hand clasped in hers, tears fell fast down her cheeks. Her companion knew she was weeping, but closed her eyes, she would not intrude on the emotion which was agitating her friend.

The music ceased, and a few minutes after, Mrs. Courtenay and Lady Boothby came to take the two friends to the drawing-room.

## CHAPTER XXIII.

THE wedding-day had at length arrived. The ceremony was to take place at an early hour, for Augustus Boothby and his bride had many miles to travel before evening. We tarry not to give an elaborate account of Maud's wedding dress, or of the wedding breakfast. Her only bridesmaid was Dora Gibson, but the Raymonds, Mrs. Gibson, Sir Harry, Lady Boothby, and Mrs. Courtenay, accompanied them to church; General Ryan gave the bride away.

Cecil Woodhouse could not absent himself, but not a trace of the fearful emotion agitating his breast was visible in his countenance. It was true he looked very pale—deathly pale—but that was all, and this passed unheeded as, with head bent over his prayer-book, he knelt at the altar rails.

The ceremony was over, and those two highly-gifted ones were united until death should them part. They returned home and partook of breakfast, and then Maud retired to her room to take off her wedding-dress, and array herself for travelling, accompanied by Dora Gibson.

The latter had scarcely commenced assisting her friend to unrobe, when she broke into an uncontrollable fit of weeping, for she was unable to disguise her deep sorrow at the anticipation of the long separation she knew must inevitably take place between herself and her dearly loved friend.

" Dearest Dora, do not cry," said Maud, fondly kissing her.

" Oh! Maud, I shall be so lonely when you have left."

" Not so, dear girl. You forget there is one who claims your deepest love, and to him, ere very long, you will be united for ever."

" Yes, I know that; still I shall miss your

companionship. You have been more than a sister to me, and have had all my confidence."

"You will soon have one who will claim your confidence, as well as your love. Do all in your power, my dear Dora, to promote his happiness, and you will have a rich reward. Day by day you will discern some new and valuable trait in his character, as well as in his mind, and your true, warm young love will call forth all the noblest and tenderest sentiments of his heart; soothe and comfort his spirit, for, Dora, Cecil has had much sorrow."

"What sorrow, dear Maud?" asked Dora.

"That is a question I cannot answer, and one that neither I nor you must enquire about. It is enough to know that he has had sorrow. He is formed by nature to appreciate and value the pure affection of a soul like yours. May God's best blessing rest upon you. Take this ring, dear Dora, and wear it for my sake"—and she slipped a beautiful diamond ring on her companion's finger—" wear it, dearest, in remembrance of one who loves you dearly, and one, too, who like Cecil has secretly suffered much sorrow, but borne it with little patience, and been most ungrateful to God. Should we never meet again, and perhaps we may not, then send up a prayer to the Throne of Grace, that I may be forgiven for my pride and ingratitude. Will you do for me what I ask?"

"Yes, yes, dearest Maud," replied the weep-girl, "you know I will. But why speak as if you thought you should never come back again? Oh! Maud, you surely don't think this. Why should you?"

A strange, wild glance shot across Maud's pallid countenance, and it was with an involuntary impulse that she replied,

"Yes, Dora, I must say it. I have a presentiment, I cannot tell why, that I shall never return to England again. It is wrong of me to tell my feelings, but I earnestly entreat you not to breathe a syllable of what I have said to my mother, or to Cecil Woodhouse, for my presentiment may be quite groundless. When the hour comes, should it be as I fear, then it will be time enough for them to know it. Will you promise me this, Dora?"

"I faithfully promise not to mention your suspicion to any one; but surely, dear Maud, this melancholy foreboding of your fate must be caused only by a temporary depression of spirits, or some slight physical disarrangement. I will not, cannot believe, that we shall never meet again. The thought is too dreadful, too miserable to contemplate."

A sad smile crossed Maud's face as she replied—

"Do not weep for me, dear girl. Death will not come upon me suddenly. Even now I am preparing for it, as I ought ever to have been, but God is most merciful, and will heed my supplications; and when we meet again, my Dora, it will be, I trust, in a far better and more glorious home—the everlasting abode of the repentant sinner. Hush! hush! I hear my mother's step. Not a word to her."

Dora turned aside to the window, and endeavoured to calm the agitation of her spirits and dash away the tears before Mrs. Courtenay entered the room; but she could not get rid of the heavy weight at her heart. Maud's strange prophetic words had filled her with a great and an awful terror.

"Dora dear," said Maud, as soon as her mother had entered the room, "will you leave me? I wish to be alone with my mother."

Dora, without another word, left the mother and daughter.

"Dearest mamma," said the latter as soon as the door was closed, "I am happy to be able to place in your hands three hundred pounds for the present support of poor Blanche."

"But, my love, will you not require a portion of the money for yourself?"

"No, it will be no inconvenience to me to give it you, for after having paid for my wedding outfit and all other necessary expenses, I have quite sufficient money remaining till—till—most likely I place another work in the hands of my publisher."

As she said this a faint but peculiar smile swept over her countenance, but without allowing her mother time to reply she continued, in a quick, hurried tone, for she felt that she was speaking to her beloved mother for the last time—

"Dearest mamma, I beseech you to take every care of your health. Robert will soon return to you to be your companion and comforter, and he must find you looking both well and happy. I leave you amongst kind and affectionate friends. Now, dearest, dearest mother, I must—I must go. See, the carriage is at the gate waiting for me. Good-bye, my own mother. Remember, if ever an hour of desolation oppresses you, that the same God watches over us both, though we are in far distant lands the same eye will be upon us and protect us, and the same ear will listen to our prayers. Beloved mother, good-bye."

Long and passionate was the embrace in which the mother and daughter held each other. Tears flowed plentifully from the eyes of both, for the parting for an indefinite period was no slight trial, still a happy smile rested on the mother's lips, as she thought the young bride was going forth with joy, and hope, and gladness in her heart.

At length Lady Boothby came gently into the room, saying—

" My dear Maud, I am sorry to disturb you; but the time has come for you to take leave of us all."

The mother and daughter essayed to speak, but a choking sensation in the throat prevented the utterance of a single word. Again they embraced, and Maud hastily left the room. Hurried were the farewells of all. Dora clung to her as if she would not be parted, for she alone knew the presentiment in the bride's mind of her own and her husband's fate. Sir Harry, General Ryan, Augustus, and Cecil Woodhouse were in the parlour. Maud held out her hand to the latter, saying—

" Good-bye, Cecil," and a faint smile crossed her countenance. " You will take care of poor mamma; do not allow her to be too much alone. Good-bye—God bless you!"

"God bless you, Maud; I will do all you wish." Then lowering his voice to a whisper, as he bent over her and kissed her forehead, added: "Blessings on you and your husband. May the God of goodness preserve you both from all sorrow. Good-bye."

Maud turned to Sir Harry; they fondly embraced each other, and the former's lip trembled as he bade her farewell. A fatherly kiss, and a clasp to the heart from her old and valued friend, General Ryan, and a fervent blessing from his aged lips, and then her husband took her hand and led her from her home. A wave of their hands to those assembled at the door and windows, the carriage door was closed, and they were whirled rapidly away to the railway station.

It was evening ere they reached London, where they intended remaining only a single day and proceed the following morning to the Continent, spending a day or two in Paris, and then on to Marseilles, there to embark for Alexandria.

\* \* \* \* \* \*

We have little more to add. Augustus Boothby and his wife were absent two years, visiting all the glories of the East, laying in a large store of knowledge. They visited ancient Egypt, Syria, Jerusalem, Damascus, the ruins of Balbec and Palmyra, and in fact, all the places of celebrity in Persia, Asia Minor, Greece, Italy, and Athens, searching the libraries of the various monasteries, and after a short stay at Naples, returned to England, where they were fondly welcomed by Sir Harry and Lady Boothby, Mrs. Courtenay, &c., Maud acknowledging with happy smiles her thankfulness that her presentiment of death or any other evil had proved a delusion.

During their two years absence Nelly Briggs had died. Mrs. Courtenay had left Belle Vue, and hired a small cottage at Easton, and taken Blanche to reside with her, who truly penitent, proved a source of much comfort to her aunt. General Ryan had gone to live with the Raymonds at Easton. Cecil Woodhouse had married Dora Gibson, and they were living happily at Pentlow Hall, the former having schooled his heart to think of Maud with the tender affection of a brother, rather than with the ardent love he formerly felt for her. The birth of a little girl delighted both parents, which Dora, with her husband's willing consent, named Maud.

Mrs. Raymond and her kind hearted husband continued at Easton, and their house was ever the centre of attraction to the principal *dramatis personæ* of our tale.

THE END.

T. C. NEWBY, 30, Welbeck Street, Cavendish Square, London.